Rosana told me things I didn't know, and I didn't think that in a short description of twelve walks around Olympia she would be able to do that.

If, let's say, you are newly moved here, then here's how to pass quickly for a native. Take Hart's walks. And practice saying this: "You know, when it doesn't rain for five whole days, I just don't feel right."

Vance Horne, longtime roving
reporter for the *Olympian*

I'm a native of Olympia, and I've been on every single 'walk' Rosana has described. She writes of them in a clear and friendly way, and I recommend you take the book under your arm and investigate our lovely home town with her!

Mary Ann Bigelow, Preserver of
Bigelow House, Artist, Writer

Olympia is one of the most enjoyable and interesting places in the United States to walk around. You will come across loads of history, diversity, and fun, thousands of friendly people, and the very best neighborhoods.

I am sure you will enjoy each of the twelve walks. This is a terrific guide.

Ralph Munro,
Washington Secretary of State

This book fills a real need. It can help long-time residents, newcomers, and visitors to discover all that we have here in the Olympia area.

Dean Jones,
Owner, Four Seasons Bookstore

Also by Rosana Hart:

Living with Llamas: Tales from Juniper Ridge
Llamas for Love and Money

Twelve Walks Around Olympia:

Enjoying Washington's Capital City

By Rosana Hart

Hartworks, Inc.
Olympia, WA

Twelve Walks Around Olympia: Enjoying Washington's Capital City, by Rosana Hart, ISBN 0-916289-20-6

Published by: Hartworks, Inc., PO Box 1278
Olympia, WA 98507-1278
(360) 705-1328; FAX (360) 357-9049
Non-local order line, (800) 869-7342

Disclaimer of Liability — Read This!

The author and Hartworks, Inc. shall have neither liability nor responsibility to any person or entity with respect to any loss or damage caused or alleged to be caused directly or indirectly by the information contained in this book. While the book is as accurate as the author can make it, there may be errors, omissions, and inaccuracies.

Publisher's Cataloging-in-Publication
(Prepared by Quality Books Inc.)

Hart, Rosana, 1942-
    Twelve walks around Olympia : enjoying Washington's capital city
/ Rosana Hart.
        p. cm.
    Includes bibliographical references and index.
    ISBN 0-916289-20-6

    1. Walking--Washington (State)--Olympia--Guidebooks. 2. Hiking
--Washington (State)--Olympia--Guidebooks. 3. Olympia (Wash.)--
Guidebooks.   I. Title.

GV199.42.W37H37 1995   796.5'1'09797'79
                               QBI95-20489

Library of Congress Catalog Card Number 95-94996

Table of Contents

Rosana Hart discovers that not all trails are kept up.
(This is not one of the recommended walks.)

About the author

Rosana Hart is a writer and publisher who has also been a
librarian, hypnotherapist, workshop leader, and llama
breeder. She has a Bachelor of Arts in Anthropology from
Stanford University, and a Master's of Library Science
from the University of California, Berkeley.

With her husband, videographer Kelly Hart, she
founded Juniper Ridge Press (now a division of Hartworks,
Inc.) in 1984 to publish books and videos about llamas. In
1991, the International Llama Association awarded her a
Pushmi-Pullyu Award for llama education.

After the Harts moved to Olympia in 1992, they
became acquainted with the community by doing the
research for this book and a video, *Exploring Olympia:
Washington's Capital City*, also available from Hartworks.
Rosana has been an active board member of Olympia's
Eastside Neighborhood Association.

Acknowledgments

This book has brought me in contact with many helpful and interesting people throughout the community, and I thank them all.

Jeanne Koenings stepped in during the last few months to help with the research and writing of the book. We also had some lovely walks and quite a few coffee stops together.

Two other neighbors have also been very helpful. Mark Foutch not only wrote the foreword but also edited the manuscript thoroughly. Roger Easton has enhanced my understanding of Olympia's past and has provided most of the historic photos used here.

The Resource Guide describes the publications that I learned from, but one special mention belongs here. Anyone who is familiar with local history will recognize that this book draws on the many publications of Shanna Stevenson. Her writings have saved much from oblivion and brought to life many bits of local lore.

My walking buddies have included Kathleen, David, Peter, and Clare Bellefeuille-Rice, Susan Dimitroff, Celeste Dodd, Nancy Irving, Kelly Hart, Jeanne Koenings, Becky and Walker Liebman, Jeanne Lohmann, Sharon Moore, Judy Olmstead, and Alexa and Drew Silver. Thanks to all of them for their patience as I stopped to scribble notes. My husband Kelly Hart has provided encouragement and helpful suggestions.

This book is dedicated to my dogs. Eleven-year-old Teddy Bear, my Australian Shepherd, continues to insist on the importance of walks. My Basenji puppy, Sunbeam, constantly reminds me that everything is fascinating! Both of them are good at getting me away from my computer and out the door.

Foreword

How many times have you said, "I wish I'd done that!" when you see something new and terrific? Well, my neighbor Rosana Hart *has* done it, the first-ever comprehensive guide to the lure and lore of walks in the Olympia area.

Prejudiced though we may be, Olympia residents are justly proud of our neighborhoods, our downtown, the State Capitol, and this glorious natural setting, beautiful enough to make strong men's eyes tear up a bit. Okay, sometimes it's the March wind that does it, but we all have a soft spot in our hearts for this place. Follow Rosana's guide and you will, too.

This community has a large reservoir of talent and commitment to meet every sort of challenge and make this an even better place. Rosana (pronounced "Rose-AH-na") is a perfect example. She and her husband Kelly are independent entrepreneurs. She has served on her neighborhood association board of directors and published the association's newsletter. She's a caring neighbor, a gardener, a student of history, a dog-lover, and a walker-explorer.

Using this guidebook is the next best thing to actually accompanying Rosana on her perambulations. This serenely realistic woman with the sparkling eye and ready wit is an interesting and enjoyable companion. Buy the book, choose a route, and take a walk — you'll see!

Mark Foutch

Olympia City Councilmember Mark Foutch is past president of the Eastside Neighborhood Association. A local history buff, he and his wife Bobbie own the historic Lybarger house. He has had a history of the house and the Lybarger Family "in progress" for a number of years now.

Preface

Writing this book has been a wonderful excuse to have fun. I'd say, "Gotta go to work now!" and then head out to explore the community. There is so much history and lore for every single place, that the book I was originally planning to write would have run at least 500 pages! So I cut back, keeping this volume easy to carry around. By the way, none of the owners or employees of the stores and restaurants that I've mentioned gave me anything for being listed; most don't even know they are included.

The walks in this book can be done by children, sometimes with modifications for walking abilities and interests. Several children accompanied me on walks, and their thoughts have been woven into the text. My lifetime love of walking goes back to long walks with my grandfather, starting when I was seven.

I haven't covered bicycling, as I rarely ride a bike. I have mentioned some disabled-accessible trails.

I hope that I have always said "right" and "left" correctly in describing the walks and otherwise been accurate. If you spot any errors, or want to suggest additions for future editions, you can let me know via the address or phone on the reverse of the title page.

Why walk? Getting to know my neighbors as I walk the dogs, a quick stroll downtown for errands or dinner, exploring a place I've never been before, moving my body and breathing deeply — all bring their own rewards.

When such pleasures aren't enough to motivate me, usually the eager faces of my dogs will get me moving. When even that fails, I remind myself of the long-term health benefits of walking, especially weight control and reducing the risks of heart disease and osteoporosis.

Olympia's short, rainy winter days pose a special challenge for walking. I watch for lulls in the rain, and it seems like they usually appear. Other options include walking at the malls, the YMCA, and at health clubs.

Even in Olympia, there are safety concerns associated with walking, especially for women. By choice, I usually walk with dogs and/or friends, and I learned a lot from the self-defense class offered in Olympia by F.I.S.T. (See the Resource Guide for details.) I consider that the benefits of walking are far greater than the risk of an untoward incident, given a reasonable level of caution.

Another reason for walking is to go somewhere. There are quite a few people in Olympia who either don't own a car, or rarely use one. For example, our friends Kathleen and David Bellefeuille-Rice and their two children go everywhere on foot, by bike, and by bus.

Finally, walking alone or with a like-minded companion offers a quiet time for reflection, prayer, mulling over decisions, and generally letting go of stress. I often recite the following blessing as I walk, saying it to people I care about. I think it's a Buddhist prayer, but I've had it on my wall so long that I've forgotten its origin:

> May you be happy and peaceful of mind.
> May you be healthy and strong of body.
> May you be free from inner and outer harm.
> May you live with joy and a sense of well-being.

It is my hope that this book, and the walking you do, will help you toward these goals.

Rosana Hart

Introduction: Olympia and Its History

Washington's capital city is a beautiful and interesting place, with a wide variety of things to do. It combines a sophistication usually found in larger cities with small-city friendliness. The downtown has retained its historical flavor. There are numerous good walks exploring the lovely State Capitol campus, historic neighborhoods, city parks, the shoreline of Puget Sound, and other attractions.

Olympia and the adjacent cities of Tumwater and Lacey together make up the metropolitan region. Many residents are here because they work in state government or local colleges — or at the famous Olympia Brewery — while others belong to families that came in the past or simply choose to live and work in a small city with access to Seattle, Mount Rainier, the Cascade Mountains, the Pacific Ocean, the Olympic peninsula, and Canada.

The climate draws people, too. Though it can rain for days on end, mostly in the winter, rarely do you get the kind of extreme hot and cold temperatures that are common in much of the United States.

These attractions have led people to pour into western Washington in a steady stream; regional planners expect Thurston County to double in population in the next twenty years. One factor that keeps this area from being pure paradise is that all of western Washington is in an earthquake zone that geologists believe could have one or more massive quakes in the coming decades.

The twelve walks described here will take you to all parts of the city and to several special places nearby. Wherever possible, the city walks go on the quieter streets to minimize exposure to vehicle exhaust. When a stretch on a busy street is necessary, I suggest avoiding it at rush hour. Because there are far more than twelve good walks in the region, I include a descriptive list of a number of other walks.

Capitol and Capital

You'll see these two words all over the city (and throughout this book). What's the difference?

CAPITOL: A building occupied by a state legislature. (You can remember this by thinking of the d<u>o</u>me.)

CAPITAL: The city or town which is the official seat of government of a region. (Think of <u>a</u>ll the people.)

History of Olympia and Washington

Imagine thick forests, huge trees with tops too high to see, with smaller trees, berries, ferns, and a variety of other plants growing under them... occasional prairies bright with wildflowers... wide tidal flats growing clams and oysters... rivers and streams, bright with salmon during their annual migrations... centuries-old Native American villages, where shellfish and salmon were harvested and potlatches were held. That's what the Olympia region was like just two hundred years ago.

Explorers

In 1792, British and American explorers sailed north along the Pacific coast. The American Revolution had recently ended, and the countries were competing for western lands. The American ship, *Columbia*, under the command of Captain Robert Gray, came from Boston to the Pacific coast. He explored the estuary (now named Grays Harbor in his honor), and he sailed into a large river which he named the Columbia, after his ship. These

discoveries later strengthened the claim of the United
States to Pacific Northwest lands.

The British under Captain George Vancouver explored Puget Sound, which Vancouver named for his lieu-
tenant, Peter Puget. Many places in the region were given
British names — Mount Rainier was named after a British
admiral — and the region was claimed for Great Britain.

Almost half a century later, in 1841, the naming
continued, as an American, Charles Wilkes, explored the
Southern tip of Puget Sound. The several inlets around
Olympia — Henderson, Budd, Eld, and Totten — were all
named for officers of his ships. No explorers cared what
the Native Americans called the places, though later many
Native names, or derivations of them, did come into use.

Settlers

The first American settlers arrived in this area in 1845.
They probably would have settled south of the Columbia
River, in present-day Oregon, as all other American
settlers had done. But one of their group, George Bush,
was a light-skinned African-American, and the racist
policies of the pre-Civil War era government prohibited his
even being there, let alone owning land. His friends chose
to go where he could go rather than to abandon him.
(Later, when this region became part of the United States,
Bush almost lost his land. A kind and generous man
himself, he had made many friends. They protested to
Congress, which passed an act so he could own land.)

Under the leadership of Michael T. Simmons, this
group of about thirty men and women settled near the
falls of the Deschutes River. Simmons named the spot
New Market, as it was new compared to the British
Hudson"s Bay Company located at nearby Fort Nisqually,
with which the American settlers traded extensively.

A town grew up at New Market, using the waterfalls to power a variety of businesses. In 1863, the town
changed its name to Tumwater, from a Native American

word meaning *waterfall*. (Walk #3 includes the falls and some historic parts of Tumwater.)

When the Simmons Party arrived, it hadn't yet been decided whether the region would become part of the United States or part of the British holdings. The next year, a British-American treaty established the boundary line at today's US-Canadian border.

Many other Americans followed the Simmons group north. The next year two men, Levi Lathrop Smith and Edmund Sylvester, took out a claim together on the land that later became Olympia. When Smith died two years later, Sylvester became sole owner of the land. He did nothing with it at first, going off to California to seek his fortune in the gold rush. But soon he was back without a fortune, and in 1850 he laid out the town of Olympia, named for its view of the Olympic Mountains.

Creation of Washington Territory

In 1851, there were about a thousand Americans north of the Columbia River. They began urging that the region from the Columbia River north to the border be made a separate territory from the rest of Oregon. In Olympia, speeches calling for a new territory were made at the Fourth of July celebrations of that year. Several men in the Olympia area raised the money to start a newspaper, *The Columbian*. It began in September 1852 and busily promoted the idea of a separate territory to be called Columbia. A petition was submitted to Congress.

Joe Lane, Oregon's delegate to Congress, didn't at first think that separation was a good idea, and he buried the petition in committee. But in 1852 he introduced a bill calling for the creation of the Territory of Columbia. He may have changed his mind because his friends in Salem decided that they liked the idea, too. The northern region was growing in population and influence, and the southern group realized that their power was likely to be greater if they let the north go. The bill passed the next year. Congress decided to call the territory Washington, in honor of George Washington, instead of Columbia, as desired by the settlers. It was not the last time that Congress overruled the wishes of local people.

Olympia — the Capital?

Washington Territory's first governor, Isaac Stevens, was appointed by President Franklin Pierce and arrived in 1853. He named Olympia the provisional capital. Since the outcry for the new territory had come from the Puget Sound area, he thought the capital should be placed there. Olympia was the closest harbor on Puget Sound, on the pioneer trail north from the Columbia. It offered the first newspaper, the customs house, and one of the most populated areas. Two years later, the newly-created territorial legislature passed a bill making Olympia the permanent capital.

But a number of other places in the territory wanted the honor and benefits of being the capital. For the next half-century there were periodic legislative attempts to move the capital. In 1859, Vancouver almost succeeded in gaining the coveted title, but an 1861 referendum of the voters left Olympia the capital. Another challenge came in 1889, just before statehood. In a referendum, Olympia received 25,490 votes. Ellensburg and Yakima combined had more than Olympia, but they had divided the Eastern Washington vote.

Statehood came in 1889. When the telegram came from Washington, D.C., saying that statehood had been declared by Congress, it was sent collect!

During the early twentieth century, more and more state agencies were established in Seattle. In 1953 several Olympia citizens filed suit against the governor for not locating these agencies in Olympia, and the next year the Washington Supreme Court upheld a Superior Court decision that all agencies should have their main offices at the capital city. Several years later, 105 years after Isaac Stevens' first naming Olympia the capital, agencies were spread throughout the Olympia region, including campuses in Lacey and Tumwater.

Growth and Changes

Relationships with Native Americans in the Olympia region began relatively well, but in 1855-56 there was a war. Governor Stevens had insisted that the Nisqually tribe move away from the Nisqually River, where they had fished for centuries, to a dry highland. Leschi, a tribal leader and a friend of many white people, was convinced that this would mean death for his people. In the end, people died on both sides, and Stevens reversed his insistence on the Nisqually leaving the river. Leschi was captured and hanged, and his brother murdered by a vengeful settler. These were controversial events even at the time.

In the 1870s, the Northern Pacific Railroad was approaching Puget Sound. Where the railroad came, prosperity, industry, and growth followed — and in those days, everyone was pro-growth! Wherever the railroad placed its terminus on Puget Sound was expected to become the largest city. With the tracks only about fifteen miles from Olympia, the railroad quietly bought up land on Budd Inlet, in the name of a businessman, Ira Thomas. Property values rose in Olympia.

Then in 1872 Thomas died. Rather than wait for his will to be probated, which then as now could be a lengthy process, the railroad put its terminus at Tacoma. It was a great disappointment for Olympians. Later, Olympia did get rail connections, but they didn't lead to explosive growth.

The same year, 1872, also brought a considerable earthquake. There have been two other notable ones, in 1949 and in 1965, calculated to be 8.0 and 6.5 on the Richter scale, respectively.

*Olympia in 1879: downtown is at the lower right,
and the heavily wooded area is the capitol campus.
That's a railroad trestle along upper right.*

The shoreline changed after 1911, when the slough between downtown Olympia and the Eastside was partly filled and downtown itself was enlarged by about twenty-two blocks. Originally, the Eastside had been separated from the city center by tidal mud flats, all the way south to present-day Union Street, almost to today's freeway.

The automobile was a major influence here as everywhere. In 1906, there were 763 cars in Washington. Ten years later, license plates were issued to more than 70,000 vehicles. The popularity of cars and the building of public highways led to the demise of rail and steamboat transit. In the late 1950s, the freeway cut a swath through the community, destroying the heart of old Tumwater.

In the following decades, the mills gradually closed and the city became less industrialized. Now Olympia is a cleaner and quieter city than it was in the past — and a good place for walks!

The State Capitol Campus

Washington's beautiful State Capitol campus spreads out on both sides of Capitol Way, with the places of general interest mainly to the west. People come to the campus for many reasons: to work, to do research, to lobby, to meet with legislators, to sightsee or picnic, to take a brisk walk — some even get married on the grounds!

The campus looks especially lovely in early spring when cherry blossoms are out, in the fall when the leaves show a range of colors, and in the winter snow (those years that we have some).

The Visitor Center (1)

Once you've parked (see *Access* at the end of this chapter), a good place to start is the Visitor Center on Capitol Way. Open weekdays year-round and also on weekends during the summer, the center is staffed by people glad to help you plan your visit. Many free brochures are available; one of my favorites is *Trees of the Washington State Capitol Campus,* which includes a walk.

Vietnam Veterans Memorial (2)

A small, curved wall of granite is bermed into a slight rise in the capitol campus lawn. The names of the people from Washington who died or were reported missing in action are carved into the wall, much like the famous Vietnam memorial wall in Washington, D.C. The 1,117 names don't go very high, so that children and people in wheelchairs can touch them. Next to each name is a little slot where a flag, a flower, or other item can be placed.

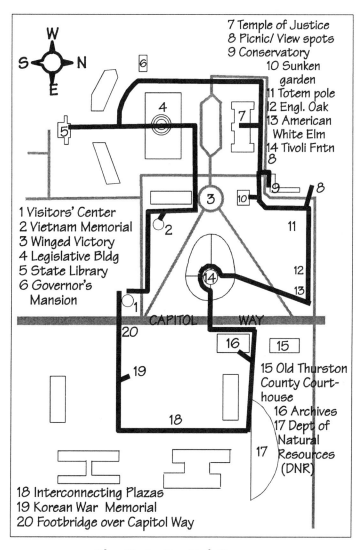

The State Capitol Campus

It's a spot for quiet reflection at any hour of the day or night, and many have found it a place of healing. People leave letters and mementos here.

The circular wall is symbolic of the circle of life, and the way the top of the wall undulates reflects both the ups and downs of life and the curves in the terrain of Washington. The one break in the circle is in the shape of Vietnam. The memorial was dedicated in 1987, and paid for entirely by private contributions. The tree beside it is one of several bigleaf maples planted in the 1800s.

On your way to the Legislative Building, you'll go by the ornate Winged Victory (3), honoring those from Washington who died in World War I.

The Legislative Building (4)

You see the dome from all over town, dominating the view in many areas, playing peekaboo in others. Beneath the dome is the Legislative Building, a grand edifice full of marble and fine fixtures.

The plans for the Capitol, the Temple of Justice, and several additional buildings began with a 1911 nationwide competition. Two young architects, Walter Wilder and Harry White of New York City, offered a plan that was less pretentious and more economical than some of the others, while also offering a pleasing classical design. Political maneuvering and World War I postponed construction for a decade, so the Capitol was not completed until 1927. In that same year, the landscaping for the campus west of Capitol Way, then twelve acres, was designed by the Olmsted Brothers of Massachusetts, renowned architects who also designed New York's Central Park and the Stanford University grounds.

If you approach the building from the north, you will walk up forty-two steps, symbolic of the fact that Washington was the forty-second state to enter the Union. The lovely bronze doors depict different aspects of Washington's historic character.

The doors at the north entrance to the Legislative Building depict Washington scenes, such as this pioneer homestead.

You can explore much of the building on your own, but if you have time, you can take a tour on the hour between 10AM and 3PM, seven days a week, by knowledgeable volunteer docents. The halls may be teeming with swarms of school children, people rallying for their cause, and well-dressed legislators and lobbyists talking earnestly with each other or on their cellular phones. Sometimes there are free musical events in the rotunda, which has interesting acoustics.

There is marble everywhere you look. It came from Italy, France, Germany, Belgium, and Alaska. If you stand in the main rotunda and look up, you'll see a five-ton Tiffany chandelier, large enough to park a Volkswagen bug inside; after the great 1949 earthquake, it swung in an ever-decreasing circle for two and a half weeks. It hangs in one of the highest masonry domes in the world.

In the middle of the rotunda, roped off to keep people from walking on it, is a large replica of the state seal. The seal was designed in 1889, just before Washington became a state. Charles Talcott, whose family still owns Talcott Jewelry in downtown Olympia, rejected a complicated design that a committee had suggested. Instead, he drew a circle around the ink bottle on his desk.

A silver dollar provided the model for an inner circle, and he printed "The Seal of the State of Washington 1889" between the circles. A postage stamp portrait of George Washington went in the middle. Later, a picture of George Washington was copied from an advertisement for a cure for coughs and colds. (The tools used to create the final version of the seal are part of a fascinating historical display you can see at the jewelry store; see Walk #2, Downtown Olympia.)

The most elegant room is the Reception Room, used for greeting foreign dignitaries, receptions, and other events. It can be entered on the tours, or you can peer in at it any time; it's located on the southern side of the building, between the house and senate chambers. Much of its teakwood floor is covered by an enormous, unique carpet.

To watch the legislature when it's in session, go up one more floor to the galleries. There is a cafeteria on the ground floor of the building where you can have a meal or snack and perhaps hear political wheelings and dealings.

The State Library (5)

Exit the legislative building on the south side, and you'll be looking between a couple of grand old buildings. State senators' offices are in the John A. Cherberg building to your left (east), and representatives' offices are in the John L. O'Brien building on your right (west). Between them you see the more modern state library, with a sculpture of gulls and waves in front. It's open weekdays, 10AM to 5PM. As a former librarian, I consider this one of the more interesting parts of the campus! Once you've entered the library, go downstairs to the Washington history room by turning left between the *Circulation* and *Government Publications* desks and then by following the signs. You can make a note of titles and request them through inter-library loan from your own public library.

Everyone is welcome to browse in the Washington Room, and there is a wealth of interesting material, from

old city directories to books recently published by
Washington authors. Adults and older children who like
such things would enjoy a stop here.

The Governor's Mansion (6)

The 1908 legislature decided that there should be a nice
place for the governor to live and to receive guests for the
upcoming 1909 Alaska Pacific Exposition. So the mansion
was built in a hurry, for $35,000, not a small sum in those
days, but the haste led to some problems in construction
which became worse as the years went by: poor plumbing,
lack of heat, and electricity which sometimes went off
when important guests were being entertained.

Finally, in the 1970s, the building was completely
renovated and expanded. A private non-profit group, the
Governor's Mansion Foundation, was formed to acquire
and care for most of the furnishings in the building; this
organization is still active today. As the house is in the
Georgian style, many of the furnishings are in comple-
mentary styles of furniture: English regency, French
empire, and American federal. The antiques in the
mansion are from the late 1700s through the 1800s.

You can take a tour if you sign up in advance.
(Often you can sign up on the day of the tour; sometimes
there is a longer wait.) Volunteers tell you about the
furnishings in each room. The tour is most suited to lovers
of antiques and history, and is not open to younger
children. If you're not touring the mansion, you can
glimpse it best after you've passed it on the walk, looking
back from the north.

The Temple of Justice (7)

Open from 8AM to 5PM weekdays, the grand Temple of
Justice is one of Wilder and White's original buildings and
the first to be completed, in 1920. The Washington
Supreme Court meets in it, and there is a law library open
to the public. There are some informative displays on the
second floor balcony.

As you continue the walk, there are nice views to the north, overlooking today's lake and bridges, and out to Budd Inlet (8). Sometimes the distant Olympic mountains are visible. The original design of the grounds called for a reflecting lake and a park to go from the state buildings down to where Percival Landing now graces the southern tip of Puget Sound. In the 1990s, great progress has been made toward the creation of Heritage Park.

The Capitol Conservatory (9)

You enter the conservatory to the sound of a fountain and sometimes to the sweet aromas of flowers. There are two benches at the end of the west wing, a pleasant place to think or relax. The annuals used all around the campus are grown here. Before Christmas, poinsettias and other winter-blooming flowers can cheer up a gray day. It's open weekdays, 8AM to 3PM year round, and also on weekends during the summer. This is a favorite spot of mine.

The Sunken Garden (10)

This garden is one of the more formal parts of the campus, and frequently has plants of seasonal interest. It used to have more perennials, but deer come up from the woods at night — hungry deer!

North of the garden is a 71 foot tall totem pole (11) carved in the 1930s by Chief William Shelton, of the Snohomish tribe. There's a wooden eagle perched on top.

There's a magnificent English oak tree (12) to the east, opposite the entrance to a parking garage. At close to 100 feet tall and 4½ feet in diameter, it's the largest English oak in Washington.

The tree just to its east is an American white elm (13) with an illustrious ancestry. When George Washington took command of the Continental Army in 1775, he did so under an elm in Massachusetts. Once Washington was elected president, the elm became a tourist attraction. In 1896, a rooted cutting from this tree was sent to the University of Washington. In time, it became the source of other cuttings, including the one that has become this tree, which was planted in 1932.

Tivoli Fountain (14)

A replica of the one in Copenhagen's famous Tivoli Park, this fountain is closed for a while during the cold months. The rest of the year it cycles through a set of patterns. Sometimes its gentle sounds are drowned out by concerts; I heard some memorable rhythm and blues here once.

You can cross Capitol Way at the marked but unsignalled pedestrian crossing here. (If you prefer, there's a traffic light to the north and an elevated footbridge to the south.) From the pedestrian crossing, head north along the sidewalk. Turn right between the state archives and the old Thurston County Courthouse (15). Now housing both private and government offices, the courthouse is attractive, with lots of marble in its corridors and a coffee bar in its basement.

The State Archives Office (16)

You enter this building from a door on the east side, into a room of displays on Washington history: statehood day, letters from presidents, state symbols, and *Remembrances from the Vietnam Memorial* — which brought tears to my eyes — were the exhibits on the day I stopped in. The State Archives Office also has historical records that are open to the public for research.

DNR: Department of Natural Resources (17)

The most architecturally interesting of the modern office buildings on the campus, the DNR also houses an excellent map shop and a good cafeteria. If you're walking during ordinary office hours, you can go in the front doors, up the wide marble stairs, and out onto one of several interconnected plazas (18). If the building is locked, you can get to the plaza by stairs.

From here, wander generally southward. People who want to get more exercise could make some loops around the various office buildings, exploring the different plazas. Eventually you'll see a row of flags on your right, with the Korean memorial nearby. En route you'll pass a lovely Dancing Woman sculpture.

As this book was going to press, I heard about a special spot I didn't have a chance to explore: To the east of the Transportation Building (which is in the SE corner of the campus), a spiral staircase leads down to a sculpture garden.

Korean War Veterans Memorial (19)

The Korean War memorial was dedicated in 1993, forty years after the end of what has been called "the forgotten war." There are larger than life size statues of three soldiers, one of them trying to start a small fire. Cloaks are wrapped around the men. There was a bite to the wind on the day I first saw it,  which made the haggard faces of the soldiers all the more vivid. There is a poetic and informative display, as well.

You can return to the Visitor Center via the nearby footbridge (20), which rises over Capitol Way.

ACCESS: Visitors coming from I-5 can follow the signs to parking, which can be rather tight when the legislature is in session, January through March or later. (The legislature begins its sessions every year on the second Monday in

January. In odd years the sessions are supposed to be for 105 days, and in even years for sixty days, but sometimes they run over into special sessions.) When the legislature is not in session, parking is easier.

Metered (50 cents/hour) parking is located near the Visitor Center, on the diagonal streets leading from Capitol Way to the Legislative Building, and at various spots around the campus. The residential area to the south of the Capitol campus has 1-hour unmetered parking near the campus and 2-hour a few blocks away, but regulations are strictly enforced and tickets are likely for overtime parkers. There are also two free Intercity Transit shuttle bus routes to the capitol campus. For information, call IT at 786-1881, or pick up schedules. These shuttles run often, all day, Monday-Friday. One of them runs from the west side of Capitol Lake on Deschutes Parkway, where there is lots of free, all-day parking.

The capitol campus grounds are open to the public at all times, but most of the buildings keep regular office hours. (Hours could change from what I've written here.) The Visitor Center is open 8AM-5PM, Mon-Fri. During the summer, from Memorial Day to Labor Day, it's also open 10AM-6PM Sat and Sun. Its phone is (360) 586-3460. The Legislative Building tours are seven days a week, from 10AM to 3PM, on the hour. Admission to the Governor's Mansion is by tour on Wednesdays only, booked in advance. For all tour information call (360) 586-TOUR. Neither still photos nor video recording are permitted at the Governor's Mansion.

The conservatory is open Monday through Friday, 8AM to 3PM, plus on weekends in the summer. The state library is open weekdays, 10AM-5PM.

There are rest rooms available throughout the campus, and cafeterias in the legislative building and in the DNR building.

WHEELCHAIR ACCESS: There is disabled access to all the buildings, and disabled parking in several spots. The capitol campus map available at the Visitor Center gives all the details.

Downtown Olympia

Downtown Olympia includes many old buildings in diverse architectural styles, a variety of shops, offices, and restaurants, and two parks: Sylvester Park, which is a centrally-located plaza and Percival Landing, a boardwalk along Budd Inlet, northwest of the downtown core.

In this chapter, I'll describe Percival Landing and downtown in one continuous walk, based in part on a brochure put out by the Olympia Heritage Commission, *A Walking Tour of Historic Downtown Olympia.* (See the Resource Guide for how you can get a copy of it and other free brochures describing walks in several neighborhoods.)

You may want to do the walk in more than one session if you get absorbed in the history, or diverted by the many tempting shops. (I've mentioned some of my favorite shops, but they reflect my personal taste, more bookstores than anything else! A lot of terrific shops and restaurants haven't been mentioned.)

Nearby Capitol Lake is described in Walk #3, but you could include a walk around its northern section here.

I found it clearest to give directions by referring to the four points of the compass. Downtown streets are slightly tilted from the true directions; I ignored the tilt. Numbered streets run east and west; north is toward the Olympics; and south is toward the State Capitol campus.

Percival Landing (1)

This is one of the first places we take our out-of-town guests. When some time goes by between guests, I find an

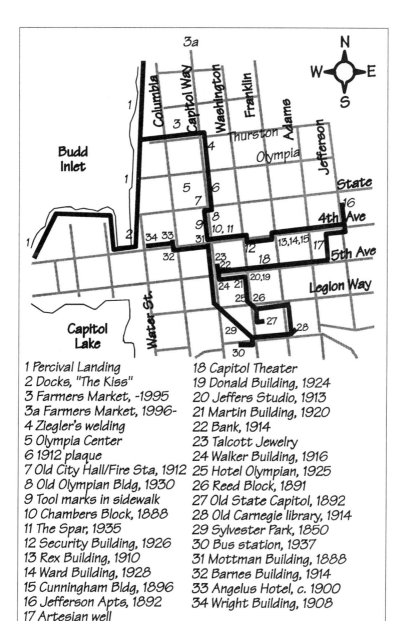

1 Percival Landing
2 Docks, "The Kiss"
3 Farmers Market, -1995
3a Farmers Market, 1996-
4 Ziegler's welding
5 Olympia Center
6 1912 plaque
7 Old City Hall/Fire Sta, 1912
8 Old Olympian Bldg, 1930
9 Tool marks in sidewalk
10 Chambers Block, 1888
11 The Spar, 1935
12 Security Building, 1926
13 Rex Building, 1910
14 Ward Building, 1928
15 Cunningham Bldg, 1896
16 Jefferson Apts, 1892
17 Artesian well
18 Capitol Theater
19 Donald Building, 1924
20 Jeffers Studio, 1913
21 Martin Building, 1920
22 Bank, 1914
23 Talcott Jewelry
24 Walker Building, 1916
25 Hotel Olympian, 1925
26 Reed Block, 1891
27 Old State Capitol, 1892
28 Old Carnegie library, 1914
29 Sylvester Park, 1850
30 Bus station, 1937
31 Mottman Building, 1888
32 Barnes Building, 1914
33 Angelus Hotel, c. 1900
34 Wright Building, 1908

Downtown Olympia

excuse to walk it myself. It's a boardwalk along the water, about two-thirds of a mile in length. If you park on Deschutes Parkway as described in the ACCESS notes at the end of the chapter, then walk along the lake to Yashiro Street (named for Olympia's Japanese sister city). Take it north to 4th Avenue, cross 4th, and go west past Bayview Market to just before where 4th becomes a bridge. Begin your walk on the boardwalk on your right.

Bayview Market has an upstairs deli area, in the NW corner of the store, with a great view over the water north to the Olympic Mountains!

Here you are at the southern tip of Puget Sound. Follow the landing around the water. You'll come to a signboard about the history of Budd Inlet, Native American activity, the Olympia oyster, Capitol Lake, and the bridges to the west side of Olympia. You'll pass the private moorage of the Olympia Yacht Club before walking down ramps to floating docks that go up and down with the tide. On the average, there's a twenty foot difference between the highest high tide and the lowest low.

These docks are city-owned, and usually not very busy. At busier times such as the Wooden Boat Festival during Mothers' Day weekend, vessels can be tied up two and three abreast. Several events take place at Percival Landing during the year; two favorites are Harbor Days, over the Labor Day weekend, when craft booths are set up along the boardwalk, and one night before Christmas, when there's a parade of boats with strings of lights and ornaments. (The date is announced in the *Olympian*.)

Go up along another ramp, and you'll be back at street level, passing by a tile map of the southern inlets of Puget Sound. Soon after that comes *The Kiss* (2), a popular

The Kiss

sculpture. One day I went by it and smiled at some tiny flowers someone had stuck in the woman's fingers. Twenty minutes later, a carnation had been added.

As you round the corner of the boardwalk and head north, take a moment to glance across the street. There's a reproduction of a famous Japanese woodblock print, *The Wave at Kanagawa,* by Hokusai. This painting is one of many pieces of wall art you'll see scattered through downtown. It was painted by a group of volunteers in 1976 under the direction of Joe Tougas; he also carved the orca whale you'll see high on a post on the landing.

The Percival Landing area was one of the first commercial piers on Puget Sound, developed in 1860 by Capt. Sam Percival. For many years, most travel to and from Olympia was via steamboats that arrived here at the landing. Since the terrain was hilly and heavily forested, roads were few and difficult. Between 1909 and 1911, the inlet was dredged. The Carlyon Fill removed some two million cubic yards from the water, and added twenty-nine blocks to downtown.

A kiosk on a pier at the landing includes photos that show old views of the port, as well as giving details of Olympia's waterfront history and the industries that used the waterways.

You'll be walking past sailing craft and houseboats. I have a friend who lives in a houseboat; she says it is quite peaceful there, and she loves the access to everything. Next there are restaurants, shops, and a commercial marina. The Budd Bay Cafe has the nicest open air dining in town, and a good harbor view from indoors.

The north boardwalk ends at a lookout tower that is open during daylight hours. Especially when the Olympic

Captain Sam Percival

Mountains are visible to the north, it offers a grand view from the top. I've been there in the winter when brilliant sun made each jagged, snowy peak stand out. There's a sign atop the lookout, describing the mountains.

Olympia Farmers Market (3)

From the lookout tower, retrace your steps south along the landing to where you see a small one-story red brick building on your left. Walk past it, and you will be at the pre-1996 site of Olympia's Farmers Market, between Columbia and Capitol Way at Thurston Avenue. In 1996, the market is slated to move three blocks north, to the end of Capitol Way (3a). The market is open Saturdays and Sundays, 10AM — 3PM, from April through December. In addition, it's open Thursdays and Fridays from May through September, and Fridays in October, also 10AM — 3PM.

Combining a visit to the Farmers Market with a walk is a favorite activity of many Olympians. The market sells fresh produce (both organically grown and not), arts and crafts, meats and fish, plants, and baked goods. There are several food and coffee stands. Often musicians are performing near the outdoor tables.

Downtown

While downtown, look up! Often the upper levels of the buildings are most interesting. Structures that have been remodelled innumerable times at street level may display more clues to their past on the top floors.

Many buildings in downtown Olympia date from the first three decades of this century, a prosperous era for the capital city. In 1949, a major earthquake destroyed many important 19th century buildings, or damaged them so much that they were later torn down. Others survived, but with simplified — and sounder — cornices and other features. In recent decades, downtown has been sprinkled with more modern structures, including a number of banks. The height of buildings is limited by ordinance, and key views of the domed legislative building are now protected.

Despite having suffered the shock that most American city centers did as life became more suburban, downtown Olympia today is a lively, enjoyable place.

Along Capitol Way

Continuing the walk from the Farmers Market: near the SW corner of Thurston and Capitol Way is Gardner's, a noted dinner restaurant. On the SE corner is Zeigler's Welding (4), an old wooden building that began life as a livery stable.

Continue south, past Zeigler's, on Capitol Way. On the west, you'll see the Olympia Center (5), a square beige building with blue windows and trim. This city-owned structure houses the Olympia Parks department and the Senior Center. It's the location for many classes and activities for all ages. Across Capitol from it is a 1912 plaque (6) embedded in the sidewalk. It marks the meeting place of the first territorial legislature in 1854. (My first draft of this sentence said, "the first territorial legislature embedded in the sidewalk." But fortunately the legislature never met *that* fate.)

Old City Hall/Fire Station (7)

On the NW corner of Capitol and State stands the old city hall and fire station, now housing a variety of family services. It's fun to see the artwork done by the children at the day-care center, which is often taped to the windows. The building was constructed in 1912, on the site of another former livery stable. It was home to the city services until 1967 and the fire department until 1993.

In a town of wooden structures and an era of smaller government, the fire department was far more prominent than the other city offices. Fortunately, Olympia never suffered the kind of city-wide fire that devastated other communities. In 1864, funds were raised for a fire engine that was shipped around the horn of

South America. It consisted of a large hand pump with two 18' handles and a 300' leather hose. A few years later, Olympia firefighters took their marvelous engine to Seattle to take part in a Fourth of July celebration. To their embarrassment, there was a fire at the Olympia jail, started by an inmate, while they were away.

Old Olympian Building (8)

On the SE corner of the same intersection stands the old Olympian building (1930). This is the first of architect Joseph Wohleb's buildings that you will encounter, but far from the last. Sometimes called "the man who designed the city," Wohleb moved to Olympia in 1911 as a young man and received his architect's license in 1919.

With its stucco walls, red tile roof, arched windows, decorative blue tiles set in the walls, and other features, the Olympian building is done in Mission Revival style, which reflects Wohleb's California background. He designed a number of buildings in that style, but he also did brick buildings, stone buildings, everything from the elegant McCleary and Lord mansions (see the South Capitol walk) to schools, government buildings, breweries, and boxy department stores. His son, Robert, later designed the present City Hall.

The old Olympian building housed the offices of the *Daily Olympian*, descendant of the first newspaper published in Washington Territory, until it moved to a larger building up E. 4th in the 1970s, from which it is still published today as the *Olympian*.

Cross both State and Capitol Way, and continue south along the west side of Capitol. About halfway down the block, notice the entryway to an old hardware store at what is now S. Vento's Photography, 109 N. Capitol Way (9). Hammers, scissors, and other items were pressed into the concrete walkway. Young children may especially like this. The window display includes historic photos and the original cash register used in the store. Next door is Browsers' Books, a used bookstore.

Chambers Block (10)

At 4th Avenue, cross Capitol Way. This will put you across from a 1922 Wohleb design, the sandstone building which has housed a series of different banks. On the NE corner of 4th and Capitol is the 1887 Chambers Block, built by A.H. Chambers, Olympia's mayor from 1886 to 1888. It originally faced onto Capitol Way. The 1949 earthquake did major damage to it, and for many years it was much plainer looking than it is now that it has been renovated and painted. Look in the windows of Sherburne's Antiques to see some prints of the building's former exuberance.

Looking up at the Chambers Block and the Spar

If you crave shops filled with charming things, detour from the walk by continuing south on Capitol past the bank, to Archibald Sisters and Popinjay.

The Spar (11)

Walking east on 4th, next door to the Chambers Block is a restaurant called the Spar, a 1935 Wohleb building. Its exterior has been redone, but go inside to look at the old sepia-tone photographs, wood-panelled walls, neon fixtures, and other Art Moderne touches. I like the newspaper ads in the hall beyond the dining area. Visitors are welcome to look around. In a political town like Olympia, a lot of intense conversation happens in these booths.

Next door to the Spar is Bulldog News; its bulletin board supplies information on local events. On the next corner, Dancing Goats is a popular spot for espresso and snacks. This part of 4th is very popular with young people.

Once a tough-looking young woman asked me for some spare change. Instead, I offered her part of a brownie I had just bought at Dancing Goats. Her sullen expression instantly melted into a pleased grin.

Security Building (12)

The 1926 Security Building — so named for a bank that once occupied its first floor — is on the SE corner of 4th and Washington. A brick building with terra cotta facing and many ornate decorations, it was built during prosperous, optimistic times. I like the griffon on the top corner. This building was designed by a prominent Seattle architect, A. H. Albertson. The lobby, open during business hours, features gray French and black Belgian marbles, with motifs from outside repeating on the ceiling. For many years, the elevator was run by an attendant and the Security Building was the most prestigious place in Olympia to have an office. You can read the list of businesses with offices there; it now houses a variety of creative and non-profit activities. Other highlights include an old photo, a descriptive history of the building, and antique light fixtures; even the mailbox is artfully done. The building came through the 1949 earthquake well, as it was set on pilings down to bedrock.

One of the shops in the Security Building, on Washington Street, is a delightful toy store for children and adults, called Wind Up Here. There are several other unique shops in the vicinity.

Along 4th Avenue

Continuing east on 4th, at Franklin is an intricate piece of wall art: "Sometimes in a Clearing," the work of artist Charles Pierce. There are three noteworthy structures in the block between Franklin and Adams, on the south side of 4th. I think they are best seen from the north side of the street. On the SE corner of 4th and Franklin is the 1910 Rex building, a Mission Revival creamy stucco with terra cotta trim (13). The 1928 Ward building, originally a

Montgomery Ward's store, is red brick with a nice silhouette on top (14). At the end of the block is the 1896 Cunningham's building, the only wooden pioneer type storefront still in existence downtown (15).

Go another block east to Jefferson Street, then turn left and go about half a block, to see the 1892 Jefferson apartment building (16). It was built by Pamela Hale, who developed a number of properties in Olympia and was also the first woman Superintendent of Schools in Thurston County. (I found it very welcome to come upon a woman whose achievements were mentioned in the history books. Not many were!) The building has been in continuous use as apartments. At this writing, it's showing its age.

Pamela Hale

As you return to 4th Avenue, glance across it and east (left) to the facades of Lynch Paints and Orca Books (another good used bookstore), then cross 4th and walk back, west, about half a block to a parking lot, just before you get to Olympic Outfitters, which was the old Union Pacific passenger station in Olympia. In the 1950s, a string of unattended boxcars loaded with tons of sheetrock rolled away from Tumwater. Gaining speed on the long grade, the cars blasted through the station without warning, hurtled across 4th Avenue, and snarled into the buildings immediately across the street. People were killed and injured. The low, newer brick buildings you see today filled the resulting gap.

Artesian Well (17)

Walk into this parking lot, and you will find water — not just any water but an artesian well of delicious spring water. There is often a line of people waiting to fill an assortment of containers. I usually stop off for a refreshing, chlorine-free drink, and my dogs appreciate the lower pipe. This fountain is an indication that much of lowland Olympia is built on springs.

Capitol Theater (18)

Continue south through the artesian well's parking lot to 5th Avenue, then turn right. In a couple of blocks you will come to an Olympia landmark, the Capitol Theater. A 1924 Joseph Wohleb design, this theater was built by E.A. Zabel, who owned a succession of local theaters from 1909 on. Before the era of film, theaters offered slides and live entertainment.

The Capitol originally included a fancy pipe organ, earphones for the hard-of-hearing, a specially glassed-in area for parents of small children, and one oversize seat for extra-large customers. In 1937, a fire caused extensive damage, but fortunately, the building was redone. The neon marquee was added in 1940. Today, the Capitol shows a wide range of films; the non-profit Olympia Film Society has an active schedule. Live events also happen on the stage. The Capitol may be shabbier than it once was, but it is still a treasured part of the Olympia scene. If you attend an event there, be sure to look around for traces of elegance. It is said to have had a resident bat at one time. The bat swooped over the seats in the darkness, adding to the atmosphere!

Looking across the street from the theater, you'll see another Wohleb building that went up in 1924, the Spanish style Donald building (19).

Jeffers Studio (20)

On the SE corner of 5th and Washington, is one of Wohleb's first buildings, the 1913 Jeffers studio, built in Wohleb's characteristic Mission style. Joseph Jeffers was a prominent Olympia photographer from the turn of the century until his death in 1924. His wife and his son, Vibert Jeffers, ran the family business for almost half a century more. Thanks to the efforts of local business-woman Susan Parrish, the Jeffers collection has been preserved and examples of it can be seen all over town in historic photo displays.

A unique feature of this building is its tall, sloping window on the north side, designed to light the photography studio below it, before the advent of contemporary lighting methods.

The Jeffers Studio, with sloping north light window on left

Along 5th Avenue

Across Washington Street, Wohleb designed the 1920 Martin building (21), built of brick from Chehalis, south of Olympia. Continuing west on 5th, at the corner of Capitol Way you come to a bank building that is now Washington Federal Savings (22). A 1914 creation, its classic style resembles Greek and Roman temples. Inside is an old-fashioned teller cage and much restored wooden trim.

Talcott's Historical Display (23)

Turn right (north) on Capitol Way to Talcott Jewelry, next door to the bank. Go in, and walk straight through the store almost to the back wall which has an 1870 map of Washington.

On your left are a series of flipboards that cover Olympia history from the very beginning to 1952. The Talcotts are an old Olympia family — Charles Talcott designed the state seal, as described in Walk #1 — and their love of the community has translated into this unique record. Visitors are graciously welcomed, whether or not interested in the jewelry for sale. There are also two display cases of antique items.

When you have had your fill of time travelling, return south to 5th, and cross it. On the SE corner is the

1916 Walker building (24), which began as a hotel with shops on the main floor.

Walk east along 5th for one block — I often get distracted here by a store called Radiance — and turn right (south) on Washington. Taking up most of the block on the east side of the street is the Washington Center for the Performing Arts, which features many outstanding live performances. On the west side, in the Martin Building, is a shop called Sara Bella, which makes charming and whimsical clothing.

Hotel Olympian (25)

At Washington and Legion Way is the Hotel Olympian, built in 1920 in a Georgian Revival style, made of reinforced concrete with a light brick and terra cotta facade. It was built by local subscriptions so Olympia would have a first-class hotel; the lack of one had been cited by other cities eager to wrest the state capital away from here. Located in sight of what was then the State Capitol, the hotel still has a spacious lobby. There were originally four dining rooms; now there is one good restaurant, the Urban Onion, along with several shops (including a bookstore, Fireside Books). The building remained a hotel until 1975; now it is low-rent senior housing. You can enter it from Legion Way, opposite Sylvester Park.

Across Washington Street is one of the earlier downtown buildings, the Reed Block (26), built in 1891. Now housing Drees, a kitchen and fine gift store, it has also been home to a newspaper and the post office.

Old State Capitol (27)

Across Legion is the old State Capitol building. It now houses the offices of the State Superintendent of Public Instruction, and is open 8AM-5PM, Monday-Friday. Enter by the stairs facing the park (handicapped entrance is on Legion Way). Just as you enter, there is a rack filled with brochures, including one that describes the building and a self-guided tour through it that you can take.

I particularly liked the model of the first state legislature building, in the west wing of the ground floor. This model was built from lumber salvaged from the building it represents.

Many faces are carved into the sandstone of the old State Capitol

The old Capitol was built in 1891-92 to be the Thurston County Courthouse. It was so used until 1901, when the state bought it to be the Capitol. The eastern wing was built right after the purchase. The legislature met here until 1928, when it moved to its present location. Fire and earthquakes have changed the profile of the old State Capitol; it used to have a tower and more conical turrets than it does now.

Old Carnegie Library (28)

Lovers of books and old libraries will want to circle around the old State Capitol to the old Carnegie library at 7th and Franklin, now the well-stocked Four Seasons bookstore, with a cafe and many activities. It was built in 1914 by a grant from Andrew Carnegie. I've seen a number of Carnegie libraries, and this is one of the nicest. It housed the city library until 1978, when the library moved one block south to its present location at 8th and Franklin.

Sylvester Park (29)

From the old Carnegie library, walk back one block west along 7th, to the one-block park donated by Olympia's founder. Since 1850, it has been the site of many holiday celebrations, concerts, performances, rallies, etc. Livestock used to graze on it. In the 1960s it was saved from being excavated for a parking garage. Margaret McKenny, one of

Gov. John Rogers stands over concert-goers in Sylvester Park.

the leaders of this movement, was also very active in the preservation of the Nisqually delta. A local school is named after her.

Walk diagonally through the park, unless you are a fan of old bus stations; there's an art moderne one (30), built in 1937, that you can examine by continuing half a block along 7th.

Leaving the park at Legion Way and Capitol Way, cross both streets, and head north, downhill, along Capitol. As you approach 5th Avenue, you're in a good position to see the elegance of the old bank (22) on the corner, and you can get a good look at the Chambers Block (10) on the corner of 4th.

Mottman, Barnes, Angelus, Wright Buildings

The Mottman Building (31), on the NW corner of Capitol and 4th, has gone through many changes since its start in 1888. It was once Olympia's premier retail establishment. On the SW corner of 4th and Columbia stands the Barnes Building (32). It was constructed around 1914, with Mission Revival elements in its style, to replace a prior building which had burned. It was a grocery, seed, and housewares store for many decades.

The Angelus Hotel (33), across 4th Avenue from the Barnes Building, was constructed around 1900, and has been continuously in use as a hotel or rooming house since then. The Wright Building (34), facing Percival Landing, was built in 1908, also for lodging, and currently houses SPEECH (an environmental group), and Childhood's End, a shop of pretty things.

Time to rest your feet!

ACCESS: You can begin the downtown/Percival Landing walk anywhere along the route, depending on **parking**. In the main part of downtown, the parking is free for up to three hours once a day. On the edges of downtown, there are metered parking places. Parking lots at 7th and Water (at Capitol Lake), 4th and Columbia, and State and Washington all have some metered parking along with reserved parking. If you are contemplating some heavy shopping, you may want to park accordingly. The hub of the Intercity Transit busses is downtown on State between Washington and Franklin, so an easy way to avoid parking problems is to catch a bus. There is a free shuttle between the Capitol Campus and downtown. The bus terminal, new in 1994, is an open design, with lots of art, including a stained-glass design of city streets.

You can also park along Capitol Lake on Deschutes Parkway, free and untimed. It's a pretty walk of a few blocks to the edge of downtown from there; this would give you a taste of Capitol Lake, or you can catch a free shuttle bus there. To get to this parking area, take 5th Avenue west out of downtown. You come to a Y where the right fork goes uphill and the left one curves along the lake. Take the left fork, where it tells you to yield. The parking on Deschutes Parkway starts shortly after this Y.

There are **public restrooms** along Capitol Lake and Percival Landing. Most of the downtown merchants reserve their facilities for their customers. The Olympia Center (between Columbia and Capitol Way, and between Olympia and State), the bus station, and the public library (just off the map at 8th and Franklin) also have public restrooms.

SPECIAL EVENTS: Artwalk, spring and fall, one Friday/Saturday; Wooden Boat Festival, Mother's Day Weekend; Music in the Park, a summer series on Wed. evenings and Fri. noons; Lakefair, 3rd weekend in July; Bon Odori, mid-summer; Pet Parade, 3rd Sat. in Aug; Harbor Days & Tugboat Races, Labor Day Weekend; Olympia Film Festival, November.

Capitol Lake & Tumwater Falls

The shore of Capitol Lake is the most popular walking area in Olympia, and with good reason: it's close to everything, and the water and lush greenery offer tranquillity and beauty. The water has many ways of reflecting what's across the lake, depending on the light and the wind. In winter, there can be a thin coating of ice on parts of the lake.

You'll see people out walking briskly, jogging, walking their dogs, or just enjoying a stroll. The route is heavily used at lunch time on nice days, or just after work, but sometimes — especially in bad weather — you practically have the place to yourself.

Capitol Lake was originally a tidal area, part of Puget Sound. As early as 1911, people suggested making it a fresh-water lake, but it wasn't until forty years later that an earth dam and concrete and steel gates were installed at the 5th Avenue bridge. Both the Deschutes River and Percival Creek (via Percival Cove) empty into the lake. It has three basins, defined by the way the water flows: the upper one is south of where I-5 crosses overhead, the middle is from there to Marathon Park (where the railroad tracks and walking bridge cross the water), and the lower basin is from there to 5th Avenue.

You'll see the ubiquitous seagulls, ducks, double-crested cormorants, great blue herons, and other birds. There's even an occasional bald eagle. You may notice signs asking you not to feed the birds; their droppings contribute to the pollution of the lake and adjacent lawns, and people food is not really their ideal diet. Unfortunately, the lake is too polluted for swimming.

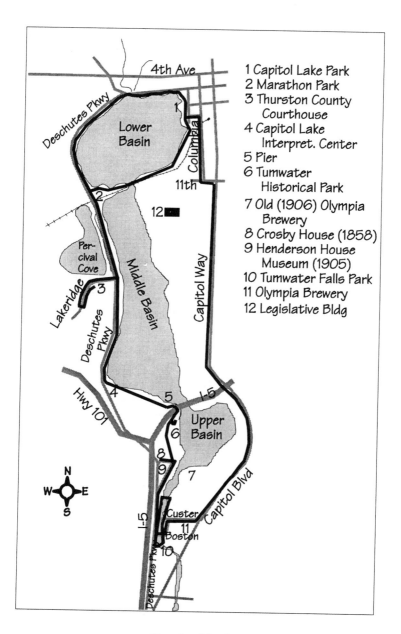

1 Capitol Lake Park
2 Marathon Park
3 Thurston County
  Courthouse
4 Capitol Lake
  Interpret. Center
5 Pier
6 Tumwater
  Historical Park
7 Old (1906) Olympia
  Brewery
8 Crosby House (1858)
9 Henderson House
  Museum (1905)
10 Tumwater Falls Park
11 Olympia Brewery
12 Legislative Bldg

Capitol Lake

I'll describe three routes (A,B, and C) plus a view loop that you could add to the second or third routes. The shortest route is a loop around the northern (lower) basin of the lake, near downtown. The second takes you along

the middle and upper basins, from Marathon Park to the southern end of the lake and up the Deschutes River a ways to Tumwater Falls. Then you retrace your steps. For the third route, you make a complete circuit of the lake, but since there isn't access all the way along the eastern shore, you walk up to Capitol Boulevard and return to the lake by walking along city streets and through the State Capitol campus, for a five-mile circle.

The second and third walks take you near the famed Olympia Brewery, where you could stop in for a tour and (if you're of age) a generous taste. The added view loop, not long after beginning the second or third routes, takes you up a hill to the Thurston County Courthouse for a pleasing view over land and water.

On parts of the walk around the lake, you'll be sharing the trail with bicyclists who sometimes whiz past without any warning that they are coming.

3A: Lower basin

Beginning at the parking lot at Capitol Lake Park, go north so the lake is on your left, through Capitol Lake Park (1) with its playground, snack bar, pier, and benches. Then you'll walk along between the lake and Deschutes Parkway. There is a dirt trail for joggers, a sidewalk, and a grassy area all along the Parkway, as well as views of the Legislative Building and sometimes of Mt. Rainier.

When you come to Marathon Park (2), enter it and pick up the footpath beyond the parking lot. (There is a grassy picnic area which invites a pause.) This path will take you over the water on a wide boardwalk paralleling a little-used railroad bridge, and then you return to the parking lot along the shore. This circuit is about a mile and a quarter.

3B: Marathon Park to Tumwater Falls

You can park at or near Marathon Park (or take the shuttle bus) for this walk, or you could do it in reverse, beginning and parking at Tumwater Falls. For a longer walk, do the added view loop, and/or combine this route with the northern loop.

From Marathon Park, head south, with the middle basin of the lake on your left, along Deschutes Parkway. This basin is the scene of speedboat races during Lakefair in July. The building across the lake, with the tower, is the steam plant that heats the State Capitol campus.

You'll see Percival Cove across the street. Some salmon are raised there. Just beyond the cove is Lakeridge Drive going uphill to the right; that's the added view loop.

Added View Loop

Cross Deschutes Parkway at Lakeridge Drive, and walk up the sidewalk on Lakeridge. When you get to the top, the first driveway on the left goes into the Thurston County Courthouse (3). (There's no crosswalk on Lakeridge, and traffic can be busy. If you don't feel like crossing, you can

Water and land alternate in the view from the county courthouse.

get the general idea of the view from here.)

Once in the courthouse parking lot, veer left and continue straight — I'm told that the lot is jammed on Tuesdays, divorce day — to where there are some benches. The view overlooks Percival Cove, the middle and lower basins of Capitol Lake, Budd Inlet, and Puget Sound. Return to the lake the way you came.

Continuing the Marathon Park to Tumwater Falls Walk

After a stretch where you walk along Deschutes Parkway, the path and the shoreline curve away from the road at the Capitol Lake Interpretive Center (4). It has historic and ecological displays.

You'll pass wetlands on your right, and you may see an old dead tree. This snag has been left there on purpose, for bald eagles who sometimes perch on it.

Next you will pass the spot where one of my dogs, Teddy Bear, rolled on a dead fish. There is no sign marking this memorable occurrence, but I can never walk past there without involuntarily holding my breath.

There are some bee hives, donated and maintained by the Olympia Beekeepers Association. From the display, I learned that honeybees must tap about 2 million flowers to produce one pound of honey.

The trail curves closer to the freeway, but the sound passes overhead and it seems amazingly quiet. Soon you come upon a pier (5), about forty feet long, that juts out into Capitol Lake. It's used for fishing, and one early morning I came upon someone practicing the graceful movements of t'ai chi chuan on it. From the pier, the open feeling of the lake is enhanced by the lush greenery that makes this region so lovely, with trees, bushes, and grasses growing right down to the water.

The water supports the growth of undesirable algae and milfoil, so just after Lakefair each year the whole lake is drained and the salty Puget Sound water is allowed to come in, killing weeds and allowing the smolts (young salmon) to make their way out of Percival Cove to the Sound. Any needed repairs to the 5th Avenue dam are done at this time, too. One friend of mine recalls how fascinated her young daughters were by the huge catfish roiling the mud when the lake was low. The lake is sometimes lowered

in the winter, if the Deschutes River is running high, so downtown Olympia doesn't flood.

Tumwater Historical Park (6)

The trail goes under the freeway and you come out at the Tumwater Historical Park.. The main route here would be to stay on the wide dirt road, but there is also a path to your left that will take you over to a couple of gravel trails that go among the woods and wetlands, out to some nice view spots. In either case, continue past the playground. There are some historical site markers just south of the playground, and another one by the water. This last one commemorates the first flour mill, built by Michael T. Simmons in 1846.

You can look across the water and see an old multi-story red brick building, the first brewery in Tumwater (7). In 1896, a German brewer, Leopold Schmidt, established a brewery here because he liked the quality of the water. The building you see was built in 1906 and used as a brewery for only about eight years, until Washington voted in prohibition. Then it was used for fruit products and other things. Now the building is in disrepair, and is closed to the public; so far, funds haven't been available for the expenses of restoration.

You'll see two paved roads as you walk out of the parking lot of the historic park. If you take Grant St., the right-hand one, it goes up a short hill to the Crosby House (8), built in 1858 and one of the oldest wooden houses still standing anywhere in Washington. Just down Deschutes Parkway from the Crosby house is the 1905 Henderson house (9), now a museum with historic displays.

If you take Simmons Rd., the other road up from the parking lot, about half-way up the hill there is a rough trail that leads down to some old foundations. Whichever road you've taken, continue now along the edge of Deschutes Parkway, up to a bridge. That's Boston Street. Cross it, walk past the Falls Terrace Restaurant, and walk down the first driveway on the left. You're now in Tumwater Falls Park.

Tumwater Falls Park (10)

This delightful stroll of about half a mile is a very popular walk. The amount of water in the Deschutes River varies with the seasons: when the water is high, the falls are more dramatic, and when it's low, you can see more of the many pretty little pools the water has carved out of the

A fish ladder beside the river

rock—and more of the foundations of early structures. In spring, the rhododendrons and azaleas are lovely.

Walk down to where the metal grates show the fish ladders beneath them, through which thousands of coho and chinook salmon come upstream in the autumn. You'll see a variety of fish ladders on this walk. At the bottom of the row of grates, there's a view point where the flowing of the water contrasts with the smooth, square walls of the modern brewery above it.

Cross the Deschutes River on the curved wooden footbridge, and follow the trail. On your left will be the river, and on your right will be a hillside with cascading waterfalls coming right down to the trail. There are cascading plants, as well, and the sound of the falls and rapids almost drowns out conversation. Indeed, for this whole walk, you can scarcely hear the nearby freeway.

After perhaps a quarter of a mile, the trail crosses the river via a sturdy wooden footbridge, next to a huge moss-covered boulder. The concrete walls that look like an old fort are part of a salmon ladder.

Just after the bridge, you can turn right down a path and some stairs to a platform. This is the foundation of the first hydroelectric generating plant for Olympia. The view of the lower falls is grand, and the spray can be refreshing on a warm day. There's also a view of the old brick brewery, partially hidden by trees.

You walk back along the west side of the river. As you pass beneath the Falls Terrace restaurant, there's a plaque commemorating the arrival of the first Americans on Puget Sound, in 1845. The list of people includes a fascinating array of children's names.

From here, you can go take a look at the fish holding tanks. At times, you can watch the work of the hatchery, not always for the faint of heart. The river is placid above the falls, and there are picnic tables and a small playground.

To finish this walk, return the way you came, back down Deschutes Parkway to Tumwater Historical Park, and then along the lakeside trail.

3C: Capitol Lake and back through town

This five-mile walk begins like the one above, at Marathon Park, and is the same through the Tumwater Historical Park. (Of course, you could begin anywhere on the circuit. If you started near the Brewery, you could end with one of their free tours! That would have you on your feet for another forty-five minutes or so.)

When you get to Boston Road, turn left and cross the river. The road curves left, up to Custer Way. You'll be walking past today's Olympia Brewery (11). This building was designed by architect Joseph Wohleb, in a simplified Art Moderne style. After Wohleb designed this brewery, he did a number of other breweries around the United States.

Across Custer, down Schmidt Place, stands the former home of the Schmidt family, who started the brewery. You can see a fine rose garden on the grounds.

From Custer, turn left onto Capitol Blvd., and stay on it. Part of the way, the path is unpaved and rather narrow. Then you'll cross a bridge over the freeway that will give you good views down to the old brewery and the falls. You'll be amazed at the height you've gained on the gradual incline of Capitol Blvd. Once across the bridge, you'll be in the South Capitol neighborhood. You could just continue along Capitol Way, or you could use the next chapter's map to vary your route. Pass the Capitol Campus, turn left at 11th, go one block and turn right onto Columbia. Take it down the hill to 7th, turn left, and you'll come out by the lake. Turn right, and this will put you at the beginning of the first walk, the lower basin loop. Follow the lower basin around to Marathon Park, and you are back where you began. If you're tired when you reach the lake, turn left and go that way around the lower basin; it's a shorter distance to Marathon Park.

ACCESS: Capitol Lake is just west of downtown Olympia and the State Capitol campus. To get to the lake from downtown, I usually take Legion, turn left on Water, and park in the lot on the right, where there is a row of free parking for lake visitors. Parking is also free and available around the lake. If you take 5th, stay left at the Y, and you'll be on Deschutes, with abundant parking. Marathon Park is another area to park in.

Intercity Transit runs a free East-West shuttle bus along the northern part of the lake, and up to the Thurston County Courthouse.

There are several restrooms and drinking fountains along the way.

To start walking from Tumwater Historical Park, if you are driving on Deschutes Parkway and coming from the north (say, from downtown Olympia), turn in on the first left turn AFTER the freeway entrance to Tacoma. That's Deschutes Way. To get to Tumwater Falls Parks, instead of turning in as above, stay on Deschutes past Boston Street and the Falls Terrace Restaurant, and follow the signs for entry to the park, which is open from 8AM to 8:30PM.

The Olympia Brewery is open for visitors every day from 8AM to 4:30PM. After a fascinating free tour open to all ages, adults are offered some free samples of the brew. Children are offered soft drinks. There's a collection of German steins downstairs.

The South Capitol Neighborhood

The area just south of the State Capitol campus has long been a favorite place for Olympians to live. Elegant homes from many eras dominate its streets, and more modest structures are tucked in among them. I always enjoy walking in this historic district, noticing a stained glass window here, a pink dogwood there. The nicely landscaped yards and well-cared-for homes provide a comforting sense of stability, order, and beauty.

All the streets have sidewalks on both sides, and the walk (with one exception, an optional section) is on flat ground. The trees are beautiful, and in warmer weather their shade is welcome.

You don't have to know anything about the history of architecture to enjoy the variety of houses. I scarcely knew a Queen Anne from a Craftsman bungalow until recently, though different houses did remind me of ones I'd seen before. There was an Uncle Wentworth, down the block was a Grandma, across the street a Dan and Gail. I might have gone on like that, but one day at the State Capital Museum store, I bought a little book, *Identifying American Architecture*. (See the Resource Guide for details.) Uncle Wentworth turned out to be some kind of bungalow, Dan and Gail a Western Stick, and I'm still puzzling over Grandma. I think her house fell into that most useful category, "eclectic."

Houses with a bronze plaque on them — usually on their front walls somewhere — have qualified for the Olympia Heritage Register. They are required to be at

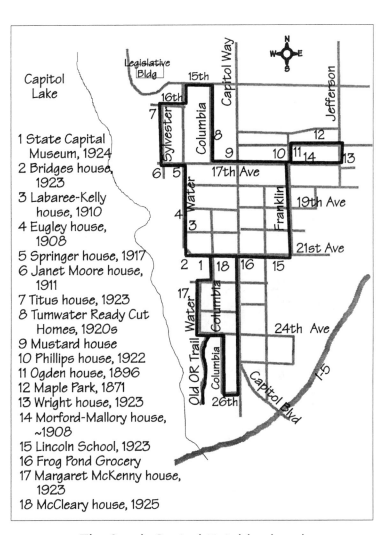

Capitol
Lake

1 State Capital
  Museum, 1924
2 Bridges house,
  1923
3 Labaree-Kelly
  house, 1910
4 Eugley house,
  1908
5 Springer house, 1917
6 Janet Moore house,
  1911
7 Titus house, 1923
8 Tumwater Ready Cut
  Homes, 1920s
9 Mustard house
10 Phillips house, 1922
11 Ogden house, 1896
12 Maple Park, 1871
13 Wright house, 1923
14 Morford-Mallory house,
  ~1908
15 Lincoln School, 1923
16 Frog Pond Grocery
17 Margaret McKenny house,
  1923
18 McCleary house, 1925

The South Capitol Neighborhood

least fifty years old and meet certain historical architectural standards, or to have an important historical association.

Northern loop (1.4 miles)

Begin by parking near the State Capital Museum (1), two blocks west of Capitol Way on 21st Ave. There is two-hour parking readily available in this area. Walk west on 21st, saving the museum for later. Next door to the museum is one of the most elegant homes in the district—the 1923 Bridges house(2), built for a Washington Supreme Court Justice and his wife, Jesse and Mary Bridges. It was designed by Elizabeth Ayer, who was from Olympia. She was the first woman to graduate from the University of Washington School of Architecture.

Turn right (north) on Water Street. As you approach the State Capitol campus, you'll catch glimpses

The Labaree-Kelly house has a distinctive doorway.

of the dome of the Legislative Building. On the right is the 1910 Labaree-Kelly house (3), serendipitously located at 1910 Water Street. Its lovely front doorway was restored by referring to historic photographs.

A little farther along, on the left at 1825 Water, is the large, turreted 1908 Eugley house (4), built in a style copied from a house on the Rhine River in Germany. Mrs. Eugley was a milliner, a popular occupation in an era when every lady owned a wardrobe of elaborate hats. From 1935 to 1967 it was used as a rooming house.

On the SW corner of Water and 17th stands the 1917 Springer house (5), designed by Olympia architect Joseph Wohleb for a local mill owner, C.H. Springer. Wohleb's career is described in the downtown walk, and he will show up again in this neighborhood.

The Eugley house

Turn left on 17th and walk over to Sylvester. On the SW corner is the 1911 Janet Moore house (6), a simple Craftsman design. Miss Moore at age seventeen became a charter member of the Olympia Women's Club, the first such club in the state. Starting in the 1880s, she taught school in Olympia for over forty years. She lived in the house with her brothers, Schooly and Lindley Moore.

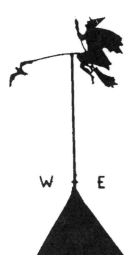

Turn right on Sylvester and walk north. One of my favorite houses is the 1923 French eclectic Titus house (7) at 1601 Sylvester, complete with turret and a windvane that shows a bat and witch on a broom! It was built for Leon Titus, who was an early automobile dealer in the region.

Here you are at the edge of

A unique windvane the State Capitol campus. Follow

around its edge by going right (east) on 16th, then left for a short bit up Water Street, then right for one block along 15th Avenue.

Turn right (north) onto Columbia Street, and you are on a charming block. There's a row of houses (8) — numbers 1528, 1532, 1600, 1602, and 1606 — down a ways on the left that were all built by the Anderson family. This group of six brothers and two sisters, all from Sweden, began Tumwater Ready Cut Homes in 1922. With a mill in approximately the present location of the Olympia Brewery, they sold precut houses all over the country and beyond. More than five hundred of their homes were built in this area, from the 1920s to the 1940s. The houses on this block were pictured in their promotional materials.

At 17th, turn left (east) and walk a block to Capitol Way. On the NW corner at 1617 S. Capitol is the Queen Anne style Mustard house (9), believed to have been moved from the State Capitol campus in the early years of this century to make way for more government buildings. It was long the home of Dr. Jack Mustard and Dr. Flora Mustard, who both practiced medicine in Olympia.

Cross Capitol Way; if traffic is heavy, there's a traffic light a block north. The neighborhood on the east side of Capitol Way has a generally less manicured feeling, and the ratio of simple to fancy houses tips to the modest side.

A fancy window in the Ogden House

Continue along 17th; at the NW corner of 17th and Franklin is the 1923 Phillips house (10), with wide columns and a deep front porch. It is a Tumwater Lumber Mills house, built for a dentist and his music-teacher wife.

Turn left onto Franklin, and at the end of the block, on the SE corner of Franklin and Maple Park, is the distinctive, large Ogden house (11), built in 1896 by lumberman Harold Ogden. According to the *Historic Property Inventory Form* for the house, when bachelor lawyers from state agencies lived there in later years, the house acquired the nickname *Empty Arms*.

Turn right (east) onto Maple Park (12) and go a block. This narrow park has historic roots. Hazard Stevens, son of Washington's first territorial governor Isaac Stevens, deeded four acres to the city for a park in 1871. In exchange, he required that the city pay for the planting of one hundred maple trees. This was done, but many years later, when the State Capitol campus was expanded, the trees were removed. In 1971, maples were again planted in the park. Today, it's a pleasant place to stroll or to sit and relax a while.

Turning right at the first corner, you'll be walking south on Jefferson. On the NE corner of Jefferson and 17th is another Wohleb house, the 1923 Wright house (13), built for one judge and later occupied by another.

Turning right (west) on 17th, the next block includes some brightly painted houses, one of them featuring some nice upstairs stained glass. Several of the houses in this block are Craftsman bungalows. The Morford-Mallory house, at 320 E 17th (14), was built for one of the first streetcar conductors in Olympia.

Turn left on Franklin. In this area on a hot summer afternoon, I noticed a woman sitting on a small porch, reading a magazine, while the glass of wine sitting on her entry walk cast a deep red shadow. I passed two neighbors pondering the ins and outs of city politics. In another block, tomatoes sprawled over half a sidewalk. Ephemeral glimpses like these do as much as the longer-lasting architecture to capture the mood of a place.

After four blocks on Franklin, turn right (west) onto 21st Ave. On your left will be the 1923 Lincoln School (15), another Wohleb design which recently received a substantial remodel. There was talk of tearing it down and replacing it with a modern structure, but people in the neighborhood and in the community of history-lovers persuaded the school board to renovate rather than destroy. The original building cost $115,607, and the recent renovation, $4.6 million.

At the corner of 21st and Washington, turn right. If you want a beverage or a snack, stop in at the historic Frog Pond Grocery (16) on the corner of 21st and Capitol. It's over seventy-five years old, and has also been known as the Lincoln Glen, Red and White, and Ron's.

Cross Capitol at the light. You may want to return now to your car or visit the State Capital Museum, as you have seen most of the noteworthy homes. The remaining part of the walk is also very enjoyable, though. (Many other streets in the neighborhood are also interesting, and there are some charming alleys.)

Southern loop (.8 mile)

Continue the walk by going south on Capitol Way, to the corner where two Capitols separate: Capitol Boulevard curves away from Capitol Way. (See the map.) Walk down Capitol Way one block, then turn right (west) onto 26th. This block is taken up by the elegant Wight and Morris houses, one on each side of the street.

Turn right onto Columbia Street, and take it to 24th, where you turn left. On your left, you'll come across Old Oregon Trail. It's a dead end, and the only hill in this walk. It goes down to a few homes and some nice views of Capitol Lake. I like the contrast in ambiance between the neighborhood above and this little road; once I saw a deer on it.

Go north on Water Street. At 2201 is the McKenny house (17), built around 1921. Born in 1885, Margaret McKenny was a teacher, conservationist, and nature lover. She wrote many books on nature, founded the local Audubon Society, and was an expert on local mushrooms. The house was built for her by her father.

Turn right at 22nd, then left on Columbia, going around the State Capital Museum. The large building on your right, facing onto 21st, that looks slightly like an elementary school is the 1925 McCleary mansion (18), now an office building. If you're walking by during weekday business hours, take a moment to go in and admire the wood-paneled walls, stained glass windows, and gracious staircase. Surprise, Joseph Wohleb was the architect for this $100,000 home.

That's $100,000 in 1920s money, about two and a half times what the Lords spent on their place next door, now the State Capital Museum. The story goes that banker Lord had once refused a loan to lumberman McCleary. When McLeary made his fortune anyway, he purposely built his bigger, fancier mansion right next to Lord's home.

State Capital Museum (1)

The State Capital Museum displays a wide variety of art, both through its permanent collection and its interesting revolving exhibits. It also has a gift shop.

The museum started out as a home built in 1923-24 for C.J. Lord and his wife Elizabeth, Olympia residents since 1890. Mr. Lord was very active in the community and had been Olympia's mayor in 1902-1903. When the Lords decided to build a new home, the choice of architect must have been easy — who else but Joseph Wohleb? He designed a 32-room house, with five fireplaces on three floors. Fine woods were used for trim. The separate coach house supplied an apartment for the chauffeur and shelter for the Lords' three Packards.

The house was supposed to be finished by Christmas 1923, but it wasn't. Nonetheless, the Lords and friends they had invited enjoyed their Christmas dinner there, bundled up in winter coats. Their dinner was served using fine china and silver on a tablecloth over an improvised plank table.

The grounds were designed by the Lords' gardener, Fred Cole, who had trained at the famous Kew Gardens in London. The grounds have since been enhanced, most recently by an ethnobotanical garden with over fifty species of Northwest plants and information about their use among Native Americans.

In 1939, two years after her husband's death, Elizabeth Lord deeded the house to the State of Washington, to become a museum. The State Capital Museum opened three years later, and has been a popular fixture of the city since. It was closed for about a year in 1994-95 for a major renovation. The coach house, where generations of Olympia children learned arts and crafts, has also had a facelift.

ACCESS: Two-hour parking is easy throughout the southern and middle parts of the neighborhood; there is also a lot at the corner of Jefferson and 16th, where the free shuttle busses stop. Be warned that the City of Olympia does pass out parking tickets, especially in the one-hour street parking area nearest the State Capitol campus.

Back at the corner of 15th and Columbia, you're just across the parking lot from the Visitor's Center. A number of public buildings on the north end of the walk have public restrooms; many of them are only open during office hours.

The State Capital Museum is open Tuesdays through Fridays 10AM-4PM, Saturdays and Sundays, noon-4PM. Admission is $2 for adults, $1 for seniors and students ages 6-18, and $5 for families. The phone is (360) 753-2580. Memberships help support the work of the museum, and there are volunteer opportunities.

Olympia's Eastside

Olympia's Eastside walk will show you grand views of the State Capitol and beyond to the Black Hills, vintage homes including one built in 1854, historic trees, a Japanese garden, the Budd Inlet shoreline and a marina, a three-acre rhododendron garden, and a bakery that's a community meeting place. The Eastside walk consists of two loops, each one a satisfying outing in itself. They are just a few blocks from each other and could be combined by ambitious walkers.

Settlement on the Eastside began in the 1850s. In that decade, a bridge was built over the tide flats that separated the Eastside from downtown. These flats, known as the Swantown slough, went as far south as where I-5 and Plum Street intersect today, and they remained unfilled until 1910. The Eastside was more rural than other parts of the city for a long time, though in the 1880s the *Washington Standard* reported, "the principal employment now of Eastsiders is staking off corner lots." Real estate mania is hardly a new phenomenon.

This part of the city consisted primarily of simple homes with a few grand ones sprinkled here and there. So although there are a number of old houses, often they weren't considered noteworthy enough for much of their history to be recorded. Many of these houses are occupied by the descendants of the people who built them. The teen-agers of one family on my block are the fifth generation in the same house. Olympia's sense of community is greatly enhanced by rooted folk such as these.

NOTE: Some smaller streets are not drawn in.

24 San Francisco Bakery
25 Zabel's Rhodies

WALK 5A:
1 Madison Scenic Park
2 Eastside Water Tower
3 Old Oregon White Oak
4 Armory, 1938
5 Old Washington School, 1924
6 Tracey house
7 Patnude house, 1893
8 Weeping Cherry tree
9 Olympia City Hall
10 Yashiro Park
11 Lybarger house, 1887
12 Yaeger house, 1884
13 White house, 1890s

WALK 5B:
14 Rudkin house, 1905
15 Sparks house, 1904
16 Byrd house, ~1891
17 Dunbar house, 1892
18 Clark house, 1900
19 Funk house, ~1906
20 Church, 1939
21 Bigelow Park
22 Bigelow house, 1854

Olympia's Eastside

Walk 5A: Eastside Neighborhood (about 2 miles)

This walk begins and ends at a park with some of the best views in the city, so you might want to bring along a picnic or snack for the end of the walk. From downtown, take 4th Avenue, Legion Way, or 8th Avenue, heading east. You'll cross busy Plum Street, where the tides still rise and fall in regular rhythms — but now they are tides of traffic. Continue past Eastside Street and Boundary (so named for being the boundary between two large historic land holdings) to Central, and turn right there. Go to10th Ave., turn left, and park in the little lot by Madison Scenic Park. (1)

Begin your walk by going up through the park. On the third Sunday evening in July, Olympia has its annual fireworks. There's always a crowd watching them here. Walk past a stage to a rambling walkway that climbs uphill among blackberry bushes. On the last stretch of the walkway, look out to the NW and you may see the distant Olympic Mountains. A bit of Puget Sound usually shows (the amount varying with the tides), and the panorama includes the State Capitol and the Black Hills behind it.

You come out of the park at the corner of Mc-Cormick and 9th. Go north (the only way you can) on McCormick, and on your right you'll see a tall gray water tower (2), visible from many points in the city. There has been water stored on this hilltop for close to a century, as a reservoir was built in the 1890s. If you walk on the concrete pavement near the water tower, you're walking on the old reservoir; to get there from McCormick, take the wide path by the octagonal pump house. The views are even better than from Madison Park, but it's not really a charming spot. From the southern end of this area, you can see Mt. Rainier to the east, framed in trees and power lines, when weather permits.

Continue on McCormick to Legion Way, and turn left. Legion between Central and Plum is known for the

One of the oaks on Legion Way; its shape is typical of the row, due to prunings

row of large, shady trees on either side of the street. Most of them are oaks, but there are some sweetgums as well.

There's a grand Oregon white oak (3) just off Legion Way, in the Methodist Church parking lot. You can see it from Legion after you cross Boundary, and you may want to take a closer look. It was planted by a settler some time after 1872, and recently became Olympia's first Landmark Tree.

At Legion and Eastside, there are two buildings of note, both Joseph Wohleb creations. On the NW corner stands the 1938 Armory (4), built in Art Moderne style from a design that Wohleb collaborated on. It was a very busy place during World War II, and is still in use today. The attractive exterior paint accentuates the building's interesting facade.

On the SE corner is the old Washington School (5), built in 1924 in Mission style. The original Washington School built in the 1890s was located where the Armory is now, so for some time people must have called this building the *new* Washington School! Now there is a third Washington School, in another neighborhood.

There are two interesting trees standing as sentinels over the school: one is a large copper beech and the other is a horse chestnut or buckeye.

An eagle stands guard above the Armory's main entrance.

Walk back up Legion to Boundary, and turn right. At the SE corner of 7th and Boundary is the Pioneer-style Tracey house (6). At the next corner, 8th and Boundary, the Patnude house (7) sits on the SW corner. It was built in 1893, during a real estate boom, but when a financial panic followed, the Oregon Mortgage Company foreclosed on the house, and the Patnudes lost it. This is a theme that will recur. There are still Patnude descendants in the neighborhood.

Walk downhill (west) on 8th. In 1994, the Eastside Neighborhood Association — with help from the City of Olympia — planted a variety of attractive small trees on both sides of 8th between Boundary and Eastside Streets. The last new tree you'll pass before you cross Eastside is a weeping cherry, chosen to be a companion to the extraordinary weeping cherry (8) on the SW corner of 8th and Eastside. A plaque under that tree says, "Dedicated to the loving memory of Max John Leitgeb [1918-1991], who lived on this corner and nurtured this tree for 35 years with the same gentle care and respect he gave his family, ensuring strong roots — yet the freedom to branch out and grow."

When Leitgeb sold the place, it was with the agreement that the tree would be protected. It has since become an official Olympia Landmark Tree. It is beautiful year-round and to my eyes at its loveliest when it blooms in the early spring.

Continue straight past the tree along 8th Avenue, and you will come to a complex of city buildings. Cross the parking lot to Olympia's doughnut-shaped City Hall (9), designed by Joseph Wohleb's son Robert. Go half way around the circle in either direction, cross another parking lot, and you'll come to the side entrance of Yashiro Park (10), open during daylight hours. This Japanese garden is a wonderful oasis of tranquillity, visual if not auditory — you do hear traffic sounds very clearly here. Bamboo, rocks, blossoms, a pagoda, a waterfall, and fish invite contemplation. Olympia and Yashiro, Japan, have an active sister city relationship. Both gates were built by visiting Japanese craftsmen and contain no nails.

Leave the park via its front gate, which opens onto Plum Street. Turn left and walk to the corner. You're at one of the busiest intersections in the city, as vehicles come and go to I-5 here. I like to remember the tides as I hurry past here. You don't need to cross the street; just turn left and walk along Union. After you pass the service station, on your left behind other buildings is a remnant of a wetland, with willows, cottonwoods, and other trees.

Union ends at Eastside Street, so go left a short block on Eastside, then turn right and walk up 10th. The next corner you come to is Boundary, and half a block south (right) on it is the Lybarger house (11), sitting back from the street on its large lot. It was completed in 1887 in the Italianate style. In 1900, with real estate values wiped out by the Panic of 1892 and in a legal and financial crisis of their own, the Lybargers turned the house over to the mortgage holder with $1200 remaining due on it.

I have a special interest in the Lybarger house: my maiden name is Linebarger, and the name was spelled a variety of ways. My Linebarger ancestors and those of the Lybargers came to the New World from the same part of Germany about three years apart. Mark and Bobbie

The White house, one of the grand old homes of the Eastside

Foutch, the present owners of the house, have obtained a Lybarger family history, and it was sprinkled with first names that are common in my family. It was eerie to find a Rosanna!

Go back to 10th and continue walking west on it. The 1884 Yaeger house (12) at 1409 10th was the first house listed with

Olympia's Heritage Register when that was organized in 1986. The house is a Queen Anne style, with Eastlake decorative elements.

When you reach the corner of 10th and Central, you can see your starting point, but there's one more wonderful house to see, the White house (13), built in 1893 by lumberman William White. Turn right on Central and go a block to 11th, where the White house is on the SW corner. The Whites only lived in their house for two years before losing it to the Oregon Mortgage Company. The 1890s were hard on homeowners.

Return to Madison Scenic Park, and if you haven't gotten enough exercise yet, you can explore the bark paths of this park.

Walk 5B: Bigelow Neighborhood and East Bay Marina (2.5 miles)

The Bigelow neighborhood is named for the oldest home in Olympia, the 1854 Bigelow house. The many interesting houses in the neighborhood, the mature trees, and some of the shrubs have all grown old together. There's a pleasing sense of interconnection.

From downtown, take 4th Avenue to Plum Street, just on the edge of downtown. Turn left on Plum (which becomes East Bay Drive as it crosses State), go two blocks, turn right onto Olympia Ave., and park somewhere along Olympia.

This walk involves two sections. The neighborhood loop is about one mile, and the walk out to the marina and back is about 1.5 miles. You might also want to walk the neighborhood, then drive out to the marina to explore it. As with several other neighborhoods, there is a free Olympia Heritage Commission brochure available, which describes the Bigelow neighborhood in more detail.

Walk east, uphill, along Olympia Avenue. The Rudkin house (14), constructed in 1905, is a lovely big house on the SE corner of Olympia and Quince, at 902 E Olympia Avenue. The house is large, with fancy columns on the front porch, and painted in subtle blues and greens. It is now used for professional offices.

After that, the most notable houses are on your left. The Sparks house (15), a 1904 Victorian cottage at 1018 Olympia Avenue, is a very sweet place. A few doors up, the Byrd house (16) is a Queen Anne style house completed around 1891. It has lions guarding the front walk. Notice too the 1892 Dunbar house (17) at 1118 and the 1900 Clark house (18) at 1126.

On the NE corner of Olympia and Puget Street, there's a mysterious old place, the Funk house (19), built around 1906.

Turn left on Puget and walk to Bigelow Avenue. At the SE corner of Puget and Bigelow is a simple church (20) which was designed by Joseph Wohleb around 1939. By this time he was doing less ornate work.

If you want to sit in a park for a spell or to use a public restroom, turn right on Puget and walk past the church and up another block to a pleasant small park, Bigelow Park (21). It includes an imaginative playground.

Whether or not you went up to the park, from Puget now go downhill on Bigelow, a rather steep block. On your right is Bigleow Spring Park, the original source of water for the immediate neighborhood. Go left where Bigelow ends at Quince Street; then make your first right turn, onto Glass Street, and you will soon come to an old house on the right, set back from the street on a two-acre lot. This is the Bigelow house (22). The first of the family to live there were Daniel Richardson Bigelow and his wife Ann Elizabeth White Bigelow. He was a Harvard-educated lawyer who was active in the creation of Washington territory apart from Oregon and in the movement to give women the vote. She was one of the first school teachers in the region. Her father, William White, was one of the few casualties of the 1855 Indian War. Her brother, also William, built the White house at 11th and Central.

The Bigelow house, Carpenter Gothic in style, was built in 1854, and it is one of the oldest frame buildings still standing anywhere in Washington. It has remained in the family, with many papers, books, and other items having remained intact. Daniel S. Bigelow, the grandson of Daniel R., and his wife Mary Ann Bigelow, have lived in the house for over sixty years, doing a great deal of public education about it. Now the house is owned by the Bigelow House Preservation Association. It has been renovated, and it will become a living history site, with

Daniel R. Bigelow

people dressed in the clothing of the period to explain the era to visitors. The Bigelows have a life estate and will continue to live in the house: your tour guide on some days will be Mary Ann Bigelow. (See the ACCESS section for details.)

Continue down the hill to East Bay Drive, cross it, and turn left. You'll soon come to a bench where you can sit and view the rugged Olympic Mountains, if they happen to be visible. Continuing along, you can see old pilings that were left in the water when the inlet was dredged, because they provide nesting sites for seabirds. Soon you will be back at the corner of Olympia Avenue, right near where you began.

To walk out to the East Bay Marina (23), turn right (west) onto Marine Drive, which is what Olympia Avenue becomes on that side of the street, and go along the path. From here you can walk out to the marina. Once you round the curve, on your left will be LOTT, the region's sewage treatment plant. Almost all of the land on this peninsula is fill that has been added during this century.

Most times of year, you can see great blue herons. Other birds to watch for include goldeneyes, horned grebes, and cormorants. Many other species have been observed here from time to time. There are always seagulls. At low tides, you can also see a lot of mud. The city has plans to restore part of this shoreline, to make it a healthier ecosystem over time.

At the marina, locked gates bar access to most of the moored boats, but at the northern end there are two floats that you can walk out on. The furthest one has my favorite view of the Olympic Mountains. Even when they are obscured by clouds, this is a special place. You can get right down at water level, watch the birds, and maybe see some sailboats come gliding in. You almost feel like you're on a boat. There are harbor seals in the area, all year.

The float just to the south of this one often has a varied array of vessels tied up at it, from hard-working fishing boats to the most elegant of yachts. As you walk back onto land, you'll see a Port of Olympia sign welcoming you to the United States.

Two Special Places
San Francisco Street Bakery (24)

This bakery is a favorite gathering spot for at least two good reasons: community and food. Its location in the neighborhood gives the area a focal point, and the food is excellent. Gene Otto, who owns the bakery with his wife, is a seventh-generation baker whose family baked in Germany and the United States. His great-grandfather came to the United States from Saxony, where the family had been baking since the 1500s. There's a plaque with the details on the wall to the left of the door, inside the bakery.

If you wanted to extend the Bigelow neighborhood walk north to the bakery, you could walk north from Olympia Street on Puget to San Francisco Street, turn right there and soon the bakery would be on the left. When you leave, walk back on San Francisco and take it down a steep hill to East Bay Drive. Walk along it back to your starting point, going up Glass to see the Bigelow house if you missed it on the way to the bakery. Going this way would create a loop of about 1.8 miles.

Zabel's Rhodies and Azaleas (25) (Open in May)

More than three acres of lovingly cared-for rhododendrons and azaleas with meandering paths make up Arthur and Peggy Zabel's back yard. Rhody lovers for some twenty-five years, for much of that time they have been opening their yard to the public during the month of May. Thousands of people come each year.

The ground rules are laid out near the entrance: no dogs, no runners, please stay on paths, unattended children will be sold as slaves. Within the forest itself, there are name cards for many of the rhododendrons, azaleas, trees, and ground covers. The occasional wood-burned signs invite contemplation. It's open in May from 10 AM to 8 PM daily. There is no charge, nor do they sell plants. From the bakery, it's .7 mile to 2432 North Bethel. Watch for RHODY TOUR sign on right.

ACCESS: These walks are accessible by various busses from the downtown terminal. Restrooms can be hard to find, but you do go past several public buildings in the first loop. There are restrooms at the East Bay Marina; the farthest north ones are open to the public. Both neighborhood walks have steep parts that might be impossible with wheelchairs.

The Bigelow House Museum is open to visitors on Saturdays and Sundays, noon to 4PM. Adults, $3 admission; children, $1. For more information call (360) 753-1215. Get a wonderful glimpse of how life was lived in Olympia more than a century ago.

Olympia's Westside

On the Westside, the land rises steeply up from Budd Inlet and Capitol Lake to a relatively level plateau of pleasant neighborhoods containing many large trees.

Western Olympia started out being a distinct community called Marshville, named after Edmund Marsh, who had the original land grant claim. Decades later, the name of Marshville was dropped, perhaps because it suggested that the land was marshy.

In 1856 the territorial legislature passed a bill which created a board of commissioners to design and build a bridge connecting Marshville with Olympia. (At the time, people rowed across.) They designed a bridge to be about 1800 feet long and 30 feet wide, with a draw span for ships going to Tumwater. It was estimated that the cost would be $3000, to be raised by private donations.

Work began, but then a white man killed a Native American. There was danger that this would escalate into a war, and so the lumber that had been purchased was used to build a stockade instead. Then there was a depression, and so it wasn't until 1869 that the first bridge was built. But the drawbridge never worked properly and teredos (maritime woodworms) feasted on the wood. In 1890 it was replaced with another wooden bridge, which lasted 25 years before collapsing (teredos again). Now two concrete bridges, both two-way, connect the Westside with downtown. The present bridge situation isn't ideal, but at least we have a new set of problems.

The westside hill was so steep and slippery that horses often couldn't climb it, especially in the winter. People had to walk up it, a process that has been described

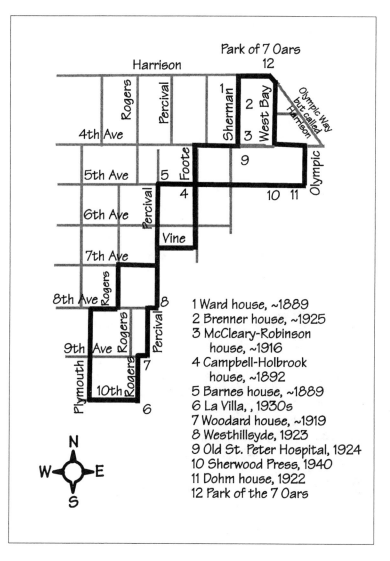

1 Ward house, ~1889
2 Brenner house, ~1925
3 McCleary-Robinson
  house, ~1916
4 Campbell-Holbrook
  house, ~1892
5 Barnes house, ~1889
6 La Villa, , 1930s
7 Woodard house, ~1919
8 Westhillsyde, 1923
9 Old St. Peter Hospital, 1924
10 Sherwood Press, 1940
11 Dohm house, 1922
12 Park of the 7 Oars

Olympia's Westside

as "like walking up a very long greased board tilted at a forty-five degree angle." The hill was regraded in 1880, and that helped a great deal. Around 1890 streetcars came to West Olympia, in a system that first used horses and later electricity. The system also connected downtown Olympia with Tumwater and the Eastside. The streetcars ran until the Depression; in 1933 they were replaced by busses.

For this walk, drive west from downtown in the right lane of 5th Avenue, which will take you past part of Capitol Lake and then uphill a little and over a short bridge. Immediately take the first left turn — it's at a place where you yield to oncoming traffic as you turn onto 4th Avenue. Go up its steep (but not muddy) hill, turn right at Sherman — the second right off 4th — and park anywhere. This walk will take you through neighborhood streets for more than a mile and a half.

The Ward house

There are three interesting houses in this block. The 1889 Ward house (1) at 137 N. Sherman, is a Queen Anne style home. The Brenner house (2) at 122 N. Sherman is a Mission Revival design done around 1925 by Joseph Wohleb for Olympia oysterman Earl Brenner, son of the founder of Brenner Oyster Company. Oysters were an important industry in early Olympia. Native Americans, who had been harvesting them for generations, sold oysters to the settlers for up to twenty-five cents a basket. J. J. Brenner was the first settler to own oyster beds. At first he had to walk out to his Mud Bay beds from his house on Sherman Street, but after a while he could afford a horse and buggy. By the 1890s his business was quite a success.

On the NW corner of Sherman and 4th is the large McCleary-Robinson house (3), built around 1916 by the son of the lumber magnate Henry McCleary.

Turn right (west) on 4th and walk a block and a half to Foote, then go left for a block. As you turn right onto 5th Avenue, notice the 1892 Campbell-Holbrook house (4); you'll get a another look at it later.

On the NE corner of 5th and Percival is the 1889 Barnes house, a Victorian cottage. Turn left and walk south along Percival for a couple of blocks.

At 7th Avenue, turn right, and walk along the sidewalk on the south (left) side of the street. At the SE corner of 7th and Rogers is one of the most interesting yards in the region. A diversity of plantings lends a sense of wildness, and the thick shade as you walk along the sidewalk is delicious on a hot day.

Turn left onto Rogers, then right on 8th and left on Plymouth to 10th. Turn left on 10th, and you are approaching an extraordinary home, La Villa (6) at the SE corner of 10th and Rogers. Ernest Meeker, an experienced builder and contractor, built this house in the

La Villa's rock walls give a rich texture.

early 1930s for himself. The stones were collected from many areas and include some large pieces of petrified wood and Tenino sandstone.

You can only get a glimpse of the house, but some recent work enables you to see the style of rockwork: the 1995 columns at the entrance to the property were done in the same manner as the house. Jeanne Koenings, who helped me with this book, and I happened to walk by while work was underway, and we learned that the rocks in the columns came from nine quarries around Washington and Oregon. Tenino sandstone was being hand-chiseled as we watched. The special beveling in the mortar highlights the stonework.

Turn left (north) on Rogers, and for the next few blocks you will be zigzagging along the top of the steep hillside. You'll go one block on Rogers, then jog a tad right on 9th, passing a nice Craftsman bungalow at 1201 W. 9th, the Woodard house (7) , built around 1919. Woodard was a teamster, a salesman, and later a candy store owner.

Turn left on Percival, and at 8th it does a little jog to the right. 726 S. Percival, at the corner of Percival and 8th, is called Westhillsyde (8). It was designed by a noted woman architect, Elizabeth Ayer, and built in 1923. I learned this from its oval sign saying *Olympia Heritage Site*, which was posted conveniently on its fence where passersby could read it. Almost always the signs are inconveniently on people's houses. The steep roof seems appropriate to the rainy climate.

There is a Spanish-style house at the SE corner of Percival and Vine. One day I asked someone working in the yard about it. I was told it was built in 1926 and was an historic landmark until it was remodeled, when it no longer qualified. It's a good reminder that there are a lot of beautiful old houses that for one reason or another aren't on the historic registers.

Turn right on Vine and go a block, then turn left on Foote. When you come to 5th, you'll get another look at the Campbell-Holbrook house (4). It's more imposing from this side, and you can see what the Heritage Commission brochure for the neighborhood aptly calls "a distinctive adjacent outbuilding."

Now turn right on 5th Avenue. As you go down the hill, you'll be passing the old St. Peter hospital (9), now senior housing. This was the second St. Peter hospital to be built in Olympia. The first one was built in 1887, on land that was developed into part of the State Capitol campus in the 1920s, thus requiring the hospital to move. It was here until 1971, when a new hospital opened in another part of town. As you pass the building, notice the stained glass windows on the upper floor of the downhill section.

On your right, you'll pass a sign for the Sherwood Press (11), and you can glance up the driveway at the building built in 1940 by Olympia printer Jocelyn Dohm and her father, from a design by her sister Phyllis Dohm Mueller, who also designed the Kornmesser house around the corner at 407 Olympic Way. Next door to the press is the Dohm house (12), built around 1922 for their parents.

There's a view of Budd Inlet as you turn the corner onto Olympic Way. When you get to 4th, go left, uphill. At West Bay, turn right and go along it to Harrison. Cross at the light, and you will be at the Park of the Seven Oars.

It's a new park that the numerous vehicular travelers can glance at briefly and a place for westside

The Park of the Seven Oars was inspired by this photo, taken at Priest Point Park in the 1890s. Only 6 oars came out clearly in this reproduction; the handle of the 7th can be seen on the far left. (Bigelow Family collection.)

pedestrians coming from downtown to catch their breath and gaze at the mountain, the Capitol, the water. The park itself has a simplicity: lawn, rounded boulders, a few benches, curving patterns in paving tiles. Seven large oars in a row rise above you.

The oars could be a puzzle if you didn't notice the placard on a boulder by Harrison Boulevard. There's an 1890s photograph of a group of young women holding up seven oars. The park is described as honoring the connection between water and our way of life. Its theme is developed by the water you can see, the logs piled up at the Port of Olympia, and — just across the street — the boat repair establishment.

Crossing Harrison again at the light, go uphill on it to the steep flight of steps on your left. They take you up to Sherman, where you began.

ACCESS: I found no restrooms on this walk; the nearest would be the public ones at Capitol Lake, described in the downtown walk. Parking is easy, and the walk could begin anywhere along the loop. This walk wouldn't be suitable for wheelchairs.

Priest Point Park

Priest Point Park includes more than 250 acres of Northwest woods with a mile of shoreline on Budd Inlet, just on the north edge of the city. Olympia is fortunate to have it: if history had taken some different turns, this land could easily have been filled with more water-view homes.

The park is named for the priests who had a mission there from 1848 to 1860, the Catholic Missionaries of the Oblates of Mary Immaculate, from France. Father Pascal Ricard received a half-section of land under a Donation Land Claim. The part used by the Native Americans in the mission era was north of Ellis Cove, where there were schools, homes, and a cemetery. In 1906, the land was given to the city for a park.

According to one of the many informative sign-boards in the park, traditionally many Native American people had come to the Priest Point Park area not only for the plentiful salmon and clams, but also to exchange goods with others. The area was called Ts!u'lyad in the Squaxin language. Once the mission opened, many native people stopped going there.

The park offers good walking, a variety of picnic areas, children's play areas (including a wading pond), beach access, and a rose garden. To get to Priest Point Park from downtown, go east to Plum Street and turn left. Plum becomes East Bay Drive, and you'll be going along the water on your left. About 1.6 miles from the corner of East Bay and State, there's a right turn that's marked "Priest Point Park." Take that, wind around past the Samarkand Rose Garden, and then turn left onto a bridge that goes over the road, where the sign says "South Exit."

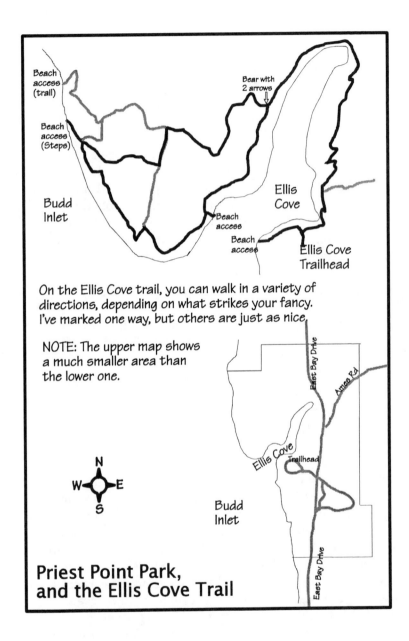

On the Ellis Cove trail, you can walk in a variety of directions, depending on what strikes your fancy. I've marked one way, but others are just as nice.

NOTE: The upper map shows a much smaller area than the lower one.

Priest Point Park, and the Ellis Cove Trail

Continue straight till you come to a sign that includes the Ellis Cove trail on a list, and turn right there. The road goes downhill, past the parking for a nice view spot, and curves around before you come to the well-marked Ellis Cove trailhead. An interpretive sign at the trailhead has a detailed map including the distances of different sections of the trail. A full walk is more than two miles, but even very short distances take you into nature.

The Ellis Cove trail is well-kept. I always enjoy being on pedestrian-only trails, as this is. (Dogs count as pedestrians.) The trail goes down to the cove, where at low tide you can see how Ellis Creek meanders. Then the trail continues back up along the northern rim of the park. There are interconnecting trails, which can be a little confusing. I sometimes get lost but soon get found again. In many places there are steps, and in others the trail itself rises steeply. There are usually handy railings where it's steep.

You pass beach areas, views of Budd Inlet and the distant state capitol, wooden sculptures of bears, and a variety of trees and understory plants: skunk cabbage, Devil's club with prickly leaves as large as serving platters, ferns, salal. The trail is in the woods just about all the time, passing under tall cedars and maples, with some trees as old as 125 years. There are some yew trees.

Even on a bright summer day, the walk is mostly shady. There are around 650 different species of plants and animals in the park.

Beware of two plants: nettles are along the edge of the trails in places, and they can cause itching for a

Devil's club

while if you brush against them. Poison oak is less common and more formidable. There is little of it in western Washington, but still I'm amazed at how few people around Olympia even can recognize it. If people brush up against it, its oil can leading to itching for days or weeks. I've gotten it from my

Poison oak, like poison ivy in other places, has three leaves together, usually shiny. Very pretty in the fall!

dogs at times. Fortunately, there is a product called Tecnu that removes the oils and reduces the itching. Strong soap (like Fels Naptha) is also useful.

I noticed poison oak in two locations in the park: both were near the salt water, which is where it seems to grow in this region. One area was by an interpretive sign called *The Forest Around Us*, and the other was at a view lookout just beyond that. Neither were on the main trail.

There are several interpretive signs. One included the statement that a salmon can swim 4000 miles in a year! Other signs tell about the marine birds and the forest itself. The signs include poetry, quotes, and illustrations. I thought they were beautiful, educational, and entertaining. The signs themselves are made in a special porcelain on steel process, by Winsor Signs, a local small business that makes signs for parks, zoos,

Whether the steps lead to the beach or directly into the water depends on the tides!

and other such facilities all around the world.

There is beach access in several places (see the map) and you can stroll along the shore. To the north of the park, the beach becomes private, and there are signs indicating this. I like to gaze across Budd Inlet from the beach. The mills you see on the opposite shore are a reminder of the many mills that were once a central part of Olympia's economy.

I've marked a suggested route on the map, but you could go other ways just as well. With all the up and down, this is a terrific walk for stretching your legs! If you did it frequently, you'd have good strong legs — and a feeling for the cycles of change in the Northwest woods.

ACCESS: Priest Point Park is open daily from 6AM to 10PM year around, and it's free. There are restrooms by the road. There are drinking fountains by the playground and the rose garden; also, there is water in the outdoor kitchens.

For walking, wear running shoes with good traction; even so, after a rain, steep parts can be slick.

At low tide you can see land way out but it's really more like mud, and the very wet mud can act like quicksand, so wading isn't as safe as you might think. Every year the fire department has to rescue people who get stuck.

Signs in many languages warn that the shellfish can be contaminated.

As in any park nowadays, women walking alone need to be cautious. One friend of mine, who does walk there alone with her dog, said she notices who is hanging around the park, including whether any men are lounging alone in their cars.

There's a sign proclaiming no jogging, running, or bicycling on the Ellis Cove trail, and then above it another sign says that jogging *is* okay from June to September, though not in groups. Throughout the park, pets on leash are fine.

There are other walks in the park, including on the eastern side of East Bay Drive.

Watershed Park

Over a hundred acres — 117, to be exact — of forest and stream tucked into the midst of city life, Olympia's Watershed Park is a good place for a relaxing walk with a friend. It also offers lessons in ecology and history.

This area and artesian wells nearby provided the city's water supply from 1914 until the late 1930s; there are still a few remnants of the old waterworks here and there in the park. In 1955, the people of Olympia passed a ballot measure to save this woodland area from development. More than twenty years later, a trail was constructed by the city with the assistance of Olympia High School students. The trail makes a loop of about a mile and a half, taking you under majestic trees — some old growth — and over stream crossings. It's named for G. Eldon Marshall, who was Olympia's chief administrative officer for over three decades, a man deeply involved in many aspects of the community.

The park is a little south of I-5. To get there from downtown, take any street east to Plum, then turn right (south) on it. Just after you cross Union Street, you are given a choice between going north or south on I-5; choose south. Then stay in the left lane and you will go under the freeway instead of onto it. There's a sign saying "To South Olympia." This road will become Henderson Boulevard, and shortly after you come out from under the freeway, the main entrance to Watershed Park will be on your left with a parking lot.

The map shows the shape of the park. I won't say a word about north, south, east, or west, as I only find it useful to think that way when on a grid.

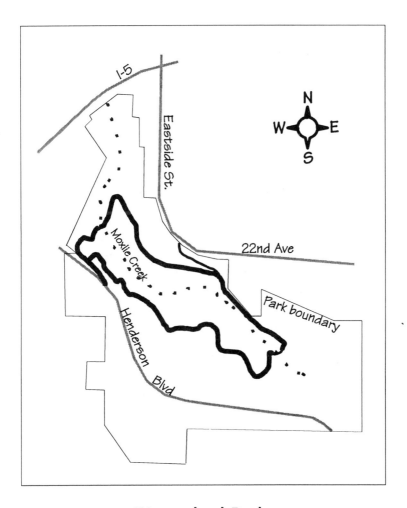

Watershed Park

A short path leads down to the loop trail. I usually turn right and walk it counter-clockwise, but there is no special reason to. Before you start around the loop, do take a look at what the path back up to Henderson Boulevard looks like, since it's not labelled.

Your walk is mostly on a trail but sometimes it becomes a boardwalk bridge over a stream or wetland. Although some logging has occurred in the past, many majestic trees either were left or have grown up since. Big leaf maple, incense cedar, and Douglas fir are present. Vine maples grow in the shade of taller trees, looking like a cross between a vine and a tree. Here and there, moss-like lichens hang elegantly over branches.

Lower down, there are salmonberries — named for the orange color of their berries — as well as huckleberries and some blackberries. There are ferns, Oregon grape, early-blooming trillium, and skunk cabbage. I've seen skunk cabbage leaves over three feet long. Their name evokes the pungent stink of their blossoms in the spring.

Animal life is varied, too. Some of the birds found in the park in the autumn (from a list compiled by the Black Hills Audubon Society) are: pileated woodpecker, downy woodpecker, northern flicker, Steller's jay, American crow, rufous-sided towhee, Oregon juncoe, black-capped chickadee, brown creeper, golden crowned kinglet, varied thrush, and winter wren. This last one, the winter wren, sings a very long song.

There are chinook and coho salmon coming home to spawn in Moxlie Creek; between 25 and 50 adult coho have been counting spawning in Watershed park in late fall months. Many of the salmon are descendants of some that were planted by schoolchildren some years ago. Consider the local part of their journey home: from the ocean they go down to the southernmost tip of Puget Sound, then near Plum and State they must enter a pipe that flows under downtown. Near Plum and Union, they must choose between Moxlie Creek and Indian Creek, then from there it's open creek to I-5, where it's another pipe section under the freeway and into the park.

You can get a feeling for the life cycles of the forest. There are several nurse logs near the trail: logs that have fallen over, decayed, and become a good place for seeds to take root. Often there will be several trees and many smaller plants growing out of one nurse log. In other places, trees have grown up on top of old stumps, with the roots of the new tree cascading several feet down to the ground in intricate designs. There's at least one large fallen tree near the trail, its formerly earth-covered roots sticking up vertically.

Having a remnant of the great forests in the heart of a city is good for us humans, but sometimes it's hard to realize just how vulnerable that forest is to our effects. Walking anywhere off the trails can cause damage.

Saplings grow from a nurse log.

The trail is more or less level for most of the loop, but one part goes up and down a hill that climbs almost to street level. My favorite times to walk in the park are in the summer, especially on a day that is too warm for a good walk elsewhere. The shade keeps things cool. I don't care for the trail after a good rain, which is to say most of the winter, as the wooden walkways and the hilly area can be quite slippery, and the trail itself can be soggy. A friend of mine said that she finds it depressing in the winter. Deep woods, short days, and lots of rain — that's the Pacific Northwest in winter! Watershed Park is a reminder of what it was all like, not so long ago.

> ACCESS: How to get there is described in the text. This wasn't designed for wheelchairs. There are no restrooms.

The Evergreen State College

The Evergreen State College, located on the northwestern edge of Olympia, is quite new for a college — the first students arrived in 1971. Many "Greeners" remain in Olympia, and help to give the city its distinctive creative character.

The concrete buildings are not lovely, but the setting is: a thousand acres of dense second-growth forest. You can take a vigorous two-mile walk on trails to the beach, do research in the college library, eat a healthy (or unhealthy) inexpensive lunch in the College Activities Building, and perhaps catch a dance performance or some live music in the central plaza, nicknamed "Red Square."

While people often comment that many of the students resemble those of the sixties, with their tie-dyed shirts, nose rings, and so on, it *is* a different era now, and these students have interests that are very contemporary: a strong environmental concern, for one thing.

Evergreen (also called by its initials, TESC) is a unique part of Washington's state college system. The students work in programs organized around inter-disciplinary themes. Unlike most colleges, there is an emphasis on working together: the students have many chances to learn how to talk in groups of people, for example. (Considering that fear of public speaking is one of the most widespread fears, this seems like excellent training!) Instead of letter grades, narrative evaluations are used. There are also opportunities for individual work. You can get to TESC by bus from the downtown transit center. By car, there are various ways: one is to take Harrison west from downtown. It becomes Mud Bay Road.

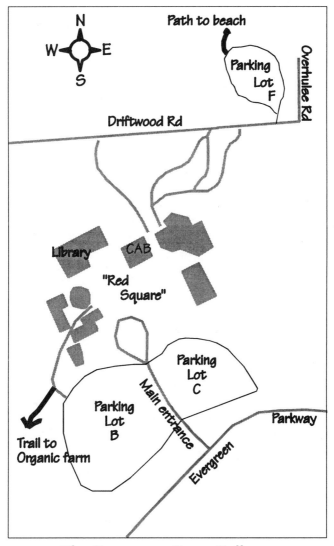

**The Evergreen State College,
Central Campus Area**

There's a sign for the right turn to Evergreen, onto Ever-green Parkway. Then from the parkway, there's a left turn that is marked as the main campus entrance. If you are there on a weekday before 5PM while school is in session, stop at the booth and pay the parking fee, presently seventy-five cents. Otherwise, parking is free. There are lots on either side of this booth, B and C, and you can park in either. One example of the egalitarianism at the college is that you will see no reserved parking places.

Because of all the trees it's not immediately ob-vious where things are. After noting where your car is, continue walking in roughly the same direction that you entered the campus, and you'll loop around past the campus bus stop, and soon find yourself at the central plaza, Red Square. If your path took you somewhere else, look for the clock tower. It's on the edge of the plaza.

Walk #12 consists of two loops, both starting and ending at Red Square; the first one is about two miles round trip, the second about one mile.

Walk 12A: To the Beach (about 2 miles)

Just north of the campus lies Eld Inlet, one of the long, narrow fingers of Puget Sound, and there is a path that will take you through deep woods to the beach. Take any of the roads or paths from behind the College Activities Building (CAB) or the recreation center, and you'll go to Driftwood Road, perhaps passing by some of the dorms. Down Driftwood a little ways to the right is the residents' parking lot F, and on its back left corner is a trail to the beach.

There is a sign posted at the edge of the parking lot, stating that there has been violence on this trail. There have been many cases of indecent exposure, and some rapes. I wouldn't walk it without at least one other person. One friend of mine who regularly walks there (but not unaccompanied) thinks that the occasional nudity on the beach attracts unsavory characters from off-campus. I asked her if she thought I should leave the walk out of the book. She felt, as I do, that the walk is so lovely it would be a pity to delete it. She said "Go in groups, and go in the daytime. Take dogs with you if you can." I would add, notice how you feel and if you are uncertain, don't go.

The trail goes through the woods. In spring, you can see a trillium here and there, and sometimes in large groupings. There are a variety of side trails. As the main trail gradually works its way down the hillside toward the beach, you get glimpses of water through the trees, glimpses that get brighter as the trees become fewer. Our trail ended at a path paralleling the shoreline; we turned left and immediately were on the beach. The view was of water, hills, and an unending row of waterside homes across Eld Inlet. At high tide, I'm not sure how much beach there would be.

The forest comes right down to the beach

As I looked back at the forest from the beach, I felt how the college is nurtured by the presence of the forest. While all the busy life of the college is going on — the research and classes, the social life — at the same time, the trees, mosses, ferns, and myriad other plants are living their lives. The forest offers a deep peacefulness to anyone who cares to notice. People who are familiar with the campus tell me that there are a number of truly magical spots on it.

We turned left on the beach and went down past a little pond. There were two more trails back into the woods. We climbed steeply up the first one, which soon joined with the second. Staying on the resulting trail took us back to the main path, and thus we returned.

Walk 12B: The Organic Farm (about 1 mile)

It's about a fifteen-minute walk to the Organic Farm from the central plaza, Red Square. If you begin at the plaza, facing south, with your back to the library, you'll see a sign that says "Lecture Hall." To the left of it, there's a gray path that will take you under the Lab II building and along an asphalt walkway to Parking Lot B. The parking lot will already be in sight when you will see a well-trodden dirt trail, going off to your right at an oblique angle. The trail takes you through a beautiful stand of second-growth firs. I walked it on one of Olympia's rare hot days, and in the open forest setting, it wasn't hot at all. There was a lot of salal and huckleberry in the under-growth.

We were soon at the Organic Farm. You can walk past the chicken house, and you come upon an attractive building called the Farm House, which can be rented out; my friend had been to parties and weddings there. Beyond it on the right are community gardens, where you can often chat with people about what they are growing. The college's organic farm is on the left. Students can learn not only about growing crops but also about the ecological and business aspects of such a venture. To return, just retrace your steps.

ACCESS: Described in the text. There are restrooms in the buildings, but there might be times when they'd all be closed.

McLane Creek Nature Trail and the Capitol Forest

West of Olympia, there is a line of dark, low mountains, visible from much of the city. These are the Black Hills in the Capitol Forest, largely owned by the state of Washington. They offer many possible walks. The most accessible from Olympia, and one of the most enchanting, is the McLane Creek Nature Trail.

McLane Creek Nature Trail

This trail is a favorite for many Olympians, but it's rarely crowded. You walk around a beaver pond ringed with wetland marsh and different kinds of forests, both decid-uous and conifer. Occasional open areas present a view of nearby hills. In the woods, you listen to the sound of McLane Creek beside you and go under the roots of a living tree. There are informative displays here and there.

McLane Creek is popular with dog owners and with joggers. Part of the trail is wheelchair-accessible and the public restroom is wheelchair-friendly. The trails around the pond include a lot of wooden walkways, useful when the boggy ground fills up with water. The walkways are covered with a kind of gritty tarpaper, which helps make them less slippery when wet or icy.

To get to McLane Creek takes about fifteen min-utes from downtown. Drive west across the 4th Street Bridge and angle right uphill. This puts you on Harrison, which becomes Mud Bay Road when you cross Cooper Point Rd. After the TESC overpass (the only overpass over Mud Bay Road), the first left is Delphi Road. Take it and go a little over three miles. The entrance to the nature trail is clearly marked on the right. The first parking area you come to is for a demonstration forest walk. Continue past it and park at the second area for the more popular beaver pond trail.

A map near the restroom shows you how the trail is laid out: there is one longer loop around the pond, with an old railroad grade cutting across the middle. I didn't include a map here as that one seemed sufficient. It's a simple layout, resembling a belt buckle with the old grade being the middle.

Wheelchair users, continue to your left from the map, and then when you get to the place where the old railroad grade is indicated with a placard, take the grade. There is a wheelchair symbol pointing to the right here. When this trail ends at a right turn with a step, you're by the main beaver dam. You go back the way that you came.

People wishing a shorter walk can also go this way. I usually continue straight at the old railroad grade, and do the full loop around the lake, excepting the grade. Some people do a figure 8, walking the grade on both circles.

An old tree root is hollow inside.

There are little walkways that jut out into the water, good for birdwatchers and just for sitting. Some friends sat quietly early in the morning near a pile of brush that indicated a beaver house. After about half an hour, the beavers came out. When a large group of lively children arrived, the beavers disappeared again.

The feeling of this walk is much more varied than that of Watershed Park. You see many of the same Northwest plants: tall ferns, skunk cabbage, salmonberries, thimbleberries, alder, Devil's club. Moss and lichen are everywhere. The bigleaf maple are glorious in the fall. Spirea, a wetland plant with purple flowers, lines the edge of the pond. If you hear a bird song that makes you think you're in a tropical jungle, it's the pileated woodpecker. In the spring, numerous salamanders hanging in the water delight the children.

Now and then you'll see a banana slug. I was walking here one day with friends when Drew Silver, age eleven, said she had been taught that if you had touched a stinging nettle, you could ease the discomfort by touching the spot with either bracken fern or a banana slug. Nobody in our group volunteered to experiment, though.

McLane Creek is a salmon spawning ground, and sometimes you can see salmon in the creek. In the fall, parts of the walk can be quite smelly, from the stench of dead salmon. Dogs love it.

The walks around the pond are described on the map as being .6 and 1.1 miles. If you want to add more to your outing, the demonstration forest loop — reached from the parking lot closer to Delphi Road — is about a mile. It has placards describing the forest management practices and different ages of the sections you go through.

Other Walks in the Capitol Forest

With the world-famous Olympic peninsula a short drive to the north, long miles of ocean beaches not far to the west, and Mt. Rainier and all the Cascades to the east, the Black Hills don't stand out. The Capitol Forest — covering some 91,000 acres — is administered by Washington's Department of Natural Resources. It is a multi-use, working forest: logging and reforesting take place as well as recreational uses. There are free campgrounds and some 180 miles of trails for hiking, horseback riding, mountain biking, and off-road vehicles (ORVs). As these uses are not exactly compatible — how many horses are happy with an ORV zipping up behind them? — the trails have been designated for different uses: the northern trails are for

ORVs, and the southern trails are for horses. Mountain bikes and hikers are allowed everywhere. During the wet season, defined as November 1 to April 1, ORVs and horses are not supposed to be in the forest at all, as a means of controlling erosion.

I have hiked in about a dozen parts of the forest, and have found some charming, serene places in the second-growth woods. But there are significant problems: ongoing vandalism of the facilities and crime. Some of the people I've met in the campgrounds were pretty wild characters. We've heard gunshots unnervingly close to where we were hiking (and not during hunting season). You can come across a logging truck or someone driving at high speed around the curve of very narrow roads.

It is easy to get lost; keep track of how you've come. There is a map, available from the Department of Natural Resources for $1; see the Resource Guide. I *highly* recommend getting the map before driving into the forest, but don't trust the map fully. Indeed, there is a warning to this effect printed on the map itself.

I found the map helpful in many ways, but several times trails no longer existed or didn't begin quite where the map showed them. Friends of mine got seriously lost in the forest, due in part to discrepancies between the map and what they found. A newer edition of the map has just come out; perhaps it is more precise.

The view from the top of Capitol Peak is sometimes touted, and Kelly and I willingly put ourselves through a lot in the quest for views. Driving ten miles or more on dusty gravel logging roads did not nourish my soul, nor did the large fenced-in electronic installations making loud hummings at the top of the mountain. Through a light haze we could see the interplay of blue inlet waters and green strips of land outlined brightly by their shorelines. That part was lovely. The view of Olympia was somewhat blocked by a long and partly clear-cut ridge between us and the city, though we could see the State Capitol and the Eastside water tower. As we strolled around the area, gunfire sounded in the woods nearby. I don't plan to return.

About four miles south of Capitol Peak (see the DNR map for directions), is Camp Wedekind, a little meadow where two roads cross in an X shape. A signboard indicates that you have reached the site of the tree-planting camp from 1947-1965. Over ten million seedlings had been planted. I imagined the workers here over the years and gained a new appreciation for replanted forests. This spot felt like the very heart of Capitol Forest.

When I was at the spot, there was only an old shelter with its fireplace vandalized, a sign saying CAMP WEDEKIND, a picnic table with one of its concrete benches ripped off, some overflowing trash cans, a parking area, and a place to tie and load horses.

The three-mile Wedekind loop trail is easiest to find near the picnic area, where you just go across the road to the horse loading area, and there's a sign saying Mima Porter trail, 17 miles to Porter. If you take that trail for about two miles, it connects with another trail, the #40, which brings you back. The junction was very clearly marked, with well-made signs, when I was there. The trails were marked for the use of horses, hikers, and bicycles, and indeed we saw hoof, hiking boot, and bike marks.

Not far from Camp Wedekind is Fuzzy Top. When the region was clearcut many decades ago, some old growth was left on this peak, simply because it was too hard to transport it. Over the years, those remaining trees seeded the hillside below them.

You have two chances to find the trail, coming from Camp Wedekind. Take Road D-1000 from Wedekind, then go left on D-3200. At a wide spot on the left (northern) side of the road, the trail begins. If you miss that, it's about half a mile to a place where several steps come down to the road, also on the left, and also with a wide spot where you can park.

Starting at the first place is the nicer walk. The trail winds down and around through mostly rather deep forest. Then it goes along a ridge and meets up with the trail from the steps. We continued and were soon up on top of a mountain. If it was old growth, I couldn't tell; none of the trees were huge, and there had been logging up there, but it was a very attractive walk nonetheless. On the way back we took the trail out to where the steps met the road and then had a relatively uninteresting trek back up the road to our vehicle. I'd go with the longer trail coming and going.

ACCESS: The McLane Creek Nature Trail is open from dawn to dusk year round, and the parking lot is open from 7AM to dusk, according to the Department of Natural Resources.

The rest of the Forest is always open. Be prepared with the map described in the text. I'd be sure to have a good supply of drinking water and snacks, comfortable shoes and clothing suitable for cold or wet weather, enough gas in the car, and other practical items in a daypack. I think it's both more secure and more fun to go with a small group of friends. Allow lots of time to drive anywhere on the gravel forest roads.

The Mima Mounds

Imagine you're at the edge of a forest, looking across a wide clearing. In the distance are farms and homes, then more forest and the outlines of mountains. You follow a trail into the clearing — and find yourself surrounded by numerous small hills, most of them a foot or two taller than you are. They are quite symmetrical and uniform in shape, with grasses, wildflowers, and some shrubs growing on them. The largest are about thirty feet across.

You're at the Mima Mounds Natural Area Preserve, southwest of Olympia, where close to four thousand of these hills occupy the 445 acres of the preserve. Many thousands more of the hills are on private land in various parts of the county. Similar mounds exist in other parts of North America and around the world. They are called by many names — *hogwallows* in Texas and *pimple mounds* in the midwest — but the expression *Mima mounds* is used to describe them all.

Nobody knows how they were formed. The first recorded theory of the Mima (pronounced "my-muh") Mounds came from the first American to travel into this region. Captain Charles Wilkes, the leader of an expedition, wrote in 1841, "They are evidently of old formation by a bygone race."

Many local residents say that the Mima Mounds
are among their favorite spots in the region. The beauty of
the curved mounds blends with the beauty of the earth
and sky around them in a very pleasing way. In a region
best known for its deep forests and water views, the Mima
Mounds provide a different experience. Sunsets can be
spectacular. There is a peacefulness at the preserve.
(However, there is a private gun club not far away, so you
may hear shots. A friend of mine who shoots there tells me
it's often busy in late summer, before hunting season.)

The walking is level and easy. The main trail, half
a mile long, is paved and suitable for wheelchairs or
children's strollers. The trail takes you out to an interesting display area, which tells a lot about the mounds and
the theories. The information display, built in the shape of
a mound, has some steps up to the top, where you are just
above the mounds and can get a good perspective on them.

The trail continues, winding between the hills. At
this writing, there are numbered plaques without the
adjacent displays, but there are plans to redo these.

You'll come to a place where a boardwalk leads to
the top of one of the hills. Near this spot, you can see a
gravel and dirt path that goes between the hills, leading to
two loops, one of about two miles and one shorter. Neither
trail is overly used or kept up, which adds to the charm.
There is also a trail that goes off to the other (northern)
side of the display; it's less than a mile long.

While the mounds themselves are reason enough to
visit the preserve, there are other attractions. The wildflowers can be wonderful. In the spring, little blue camas
blanket the hills. In the early summer, you'll see bluebells,
woolly sunflowers, and oxeye daisies, all surrounded by
the lush beauty of the grasses. As the grasses turn golden
later in the summer, some herbs flower, including spotted
cat's-ear and St. John's wort.

The mounds are good for butterfly-viewing in
spring and early summer. On one very windy May
morning, I didn't see butterflies, but I did see a soaring

hawk, and three deer running up and down the mounds. You can often hear songbirds as well.

At the time of the Wilkes expedition, most of the mounds were grassland. Canadian artist Paul Kane, who painted the mounds in 1847, wrote, "I travelled twenty-two miles through this extraordinary looking prairie. The whole surface is thickly covered with coarse grass."

The grasses send out millions of roots, some going as deep as nine feet. They hold soil and moisture, and provide an inviting environment for wildflowers and other low-growing plants, such as wild strawberries, ferns, and mosses. These plants form a thick mat which makes it almost impossible for tree seeds to gain a foothold.

Over the centuries, fires were common on the mounds: lightning would cause late-summer fires, and according to a local Native American, the area was sometimes burned to encourage the growth of bulbs, roots, and berries. Always the grasses and true prairie plants would come back from their roots.

A private fence goes up and down with the mounds.

When settlers came into the area in the 1850s, they tried to control the grassland fires and they often grazed their cattle on the mounds. These changes created conditions that allowed trees to get started. In their shade, the grass died, more trees took root, and so the forest spread. Today, many of the mounds in the county are forested, including some in the preserve. The picnic area has tables on several mound-tops, shaded by the trees.

As population increased in the county, people saw the value of saving some of the Mima Mounds for research, tourism, and public enjoyment. The present preserve was cared for by several organizations, including the Evergreen State College, before coming under the management of the state's Department of Natural Resources (DNR).

The DNR's management includes burning small portions of the mounds, a process which is expected to continue every two to four years, in an effort to control non-native plants. The most visible offender is the tenacious Scotch broom, a shrub with deep green leaves and bright yellow blossoms. It's very difficult to eradicate; some digging is also planned.

How were they formed?

They weren't formed by Wilkes' "bygone race." The *Seattle Times* listed other rejected theories: "The mounds are not Indian burial grounds, the residue of great Indian shellfish feasts, the work of ants or sucker fish, buffalo wallows, the result of volcanic upheaval or remnants of the erosion-resistant root systems of giant trees or wild cucumbers."

That leaves a variety of geological theories, and one involving pocket gophers. I've grumbled at plenty of pocket gophers in my gardens; maybe I should have been grateful that they didn't get started on mounds seven feet high and thirty feet wide!

Geological theories

The display at Mima Mounds describes one of the geological theories: it suggest that the freezing and thawing after the Vashon Glacier receded about twelve thousand years ago could have made the mounds, with their randomly sorted gravel and sand deposits. The hills aren't eroded as you might expect after so many years, though.

There are also erosion theories suggesting that either wind or water removed the soil surrounding the mounds while leaving the mounds intact, and a wind deposit theory, suggesting that the mounds were deposited by the wind around plants that have since disappeared without a trace.

The newest of the geological theories is the earthquake one. According to Andrew W. Berg, writing in a scientific journal, "Mima mounds can be produced experimentally by subjecting a plywood board covered with a thin veneer of loess to impacts that produce vibrations on the board. Experimentally produced mounds have characteristics that are nearly identical to those found in the field. This suggests that most Mima mounds formed as a result of seismic activity."

The Gopher theory

This idea suggests that ancient pocket gophers, about one foot long, couldn't burrow into the gravel, so they mounded the thin topsoil. As generations passed, the mounds would have grown larger. There are no gophers at the preserve now, though there are some in mounded prairies a few miles away. When several mounds were excavated in 1976, no animal remains were found, but a high total organic content was. All the Mima mounds in North America are within the range of pocket gophers today.

Where most geological explanations have tended to focus on the unique history of the site, gopher theorists point out that if you look at the Mima mounds in many places, they are all made of gravel, small pebbles and rocks. They don't contain heavy clay soils or large rocks. The soil beneath the mounds is always shallow, going down to some natural barrier (such as dense clay soil, rock, or a high water table). This is consistent with what you'd expect if the soil had been moved by gophers, who would leave the larger rocks alone.

Gophers are solitary animals, and the spacing of the mounds is about right for the size of territory they typically establish. As for the amount of dirt they would have to move, in one study in Texas, the amount of soil brought to the surface from its tunnels by one busy gopher came to just over two cubic yards and weighed over five thousand pounds!

I told a nine-year-old friend of mine that I was reading about the Mima Mounds theories. She was unimpressed with geology and rodents. "Paul Bunyan did it," she asserted. Whatever their history, the Mima Mounds are a wonderful place to walk and to reflect on the mysteries of life.

ACCESS: The Mima Mound Natural Area Preserve is open during daylight hours every day. There is no entrance fee. To get there from Olympia, take I-5 south to Exit 95. Go west to Littlerock on State Highway 121. Go straight through Littlerock, and you'll be on 128th Avenue. It ends at Waddell Creek Road, where you turn right and go about a mile to the preserve's entrance on the left. You can return the same way, or you can return to Littlerock and turn left onto Littlerock Rd. Stay on this, and you will come into Tumwater. Turn right on Trosper Road, and go over the freeway. Turn left at the next traffic light, and you'll be on Capitol Blvd, which will take you into downtown Olympia. The drive takes under half an hour either way.; it's faster on the freeway.   There is a picnic area, with restrooms but no water. The half-mile paved trail is wheelchair-accessible. The picnic area is fenced off from the prairie mounds, as there are no developed trails right near there, but it's just a short walk to where the trails begin.

Once in a while, the preserve is closed to the public for very brief periods while the DNR conducts controlled burns or other management and restoration activity; the burns most often take place in September. If you want to phone to make sure this isn't going to be the case before your visit, you could call the regional office of the DNR at 753-3410, or the Forest Resources Division of the DNR, the section responsible for the ecological management of the preserve, at 902-1340.

No dogs, horses, or other pets are allowed at the Mima Mounds, due to the sensitive nature of the land.

The Nisqually Delta

The Nisqually River originates among the glaciers of Mount Rainier and seventy-eight miles later arrives at Puget Sound. Its estuary has suffered less human impact than have the other estuaries around the Sound.

The Nisqually National Wildlife Refuge was established in 1974, after citizens fought off proposals to use the area for a sanitary landfill or a deep-water port. It provides habitat for hundreds of species of fish, small mammals, and birds. The state of Washington owns lands contiguous to the 2800-acre Refuge, so quite a large area is protected.

The wildlife comes first here. This is not a place to bring pets, frisbees, or bicycles. Even jogging is not permitted as it's been found to be disturbing to a number of the animals. Sometimes parts of the trails are closed to the public. This is one of the finest places around to immerse yourself in nature as you walk. Binoculars are fun to have along, especially for looking at the birds. Over 80,000 visitors a year come here to walk or to take part in education programs in the two grand old barns on the refuge.

Native Americans have inhabited this region since long before the white people came. In 1854, the first Indian treaty in the Northwest was signed in the Nisqually delta. The Nisqually Tribe continues today in the area.

Part of the present refuge was a farm for some years, and during that time a dike was built. Now when you walk along the Brown Farm dike trail, it's easy to notice the variety of habitats. Inside the dike are open grasslands where mice and voles thrive, providing food for hawks, owls, and coyotes. There are also freshwater marshes inside the dike.

Along the dike itself, you're in the woods and in brush, two more habitats. Outside the dike, you'll see the Nisqually River and McAllister Creek, saltwater marshes, and the mudflats.

The Refuge is a birdwatcher's heaven, with both migratory and local birds of many kinds. In a world increasingly developed by humans, this spot has become vitally important as a stopping place for migratory birds throughout the year.

Fish include salmon and steelhead passing through the estuary on their way upriver. Small mammals are numerous; on a recent visit, a mink crossed the path right in front of me.

Kelly and I first saw the Refuge on a cold, gray Christmas Day. I found myself thinking photographically as we walked out the dike trail. I noticed the vivid greens of moss covering a squat concrete structure; the lacy patterns of trees with little seed pods still attached; the textural richness of stiff brown marsh grasses jutting out of smooth gray waterways reflecting cloud patterns; the beaver-chewed tree; the scattered black scat containing the fur of a smaller creature.

In the past few decades, with the abundance of beautiful photographic books on natural scenes, we've learned a way of seeing which sometimes dominates our experiences. There I was moving through this place, and yet my mind was translating it all into a series of still photos!

We saw few birds and no mammals (other than a few Christmas hikers) that day, but I felt refreshed just by knowing the creatures were somewhere around. While we never got away from a steady background hum of freeway noise, eventually the silence of the place overshadowed the distant drone.

I've been back many times since, and I always feel refreshed afterwards. I know people who walk it more or less weekly, both for the exercise and just to be there. There's always something different to see, as the cycles of nature change. Some of the best wildlife watching is said to be when the weather clears after several days of rain and the animals are all busily looking for food.

I joined a bird walk one Saturday in September. The quick, sharp eyes of the experienced birdwatchers noticed things long before I did. Still, I saw crows, geese, a red-tailed hawk, goldfinches (brown at that season), warblers, song sparrows, chickadees, distant seagulls, a flicker, a small downy woodpecker busy pecking, and a great blue heron flying close by.

The trails consist of one main 5.5 mile loop with several shorter choices. From the parking lot, go to the information kiosk and pay station. Continuing along that path, you soon come to a choice.

You can go left to the twin barns, where the education center is located. Programs for school children and other groups are put on here. I've enjoyed some of their summer evening lecture series for the public. Look for the observation deck on the far side of the further barn. Going there and back is about a one-mile loop.

More often at this juncture, I turn right and go along the dike trail. Very soon you come to the entrance to the Nisqually River Trail, which runs through a riparian (riverside) woodland. There is a nicely done little brochure in a box at the start of this trail, describing its environ-ment in words and drawings. Usually I skip the river trail and continue out the dike trail. Soon you pass a path coming in from the left which is part of the Twin Barns one-mile loop.

Along here, you are on the dike, a wide and flat surface, great for walking and talking with a friend. The Nisqually River is on your right. In the rainy season, the trail can be quite muddy and I prefer boots to walking shoes. After a while you pass a trail on your left, which loops around to a photo blind. It's a nice addition to the walk, and sometimes on a shorter outing, I've used it as a turning-around point.

If you continue out the dike trail, after a while you'll come to a sign pointing you to the Nisqually River overlook on your right.

The observation tower has a great view.

The next landmark is also on your right: an observation tower just off the trail. I love the view from here, and always linger to gaze out at the mud flats, the water, distant shores and land. The vista varies according to the tide, which has a range of about 18 feet here.

My eye usually tries to skip over the houses visible on the bluff to the west, though! The bluffs are a nesting site for great blue herons, bald eagles and others. These bluffs are not part of the refuge, and there is concern about their future. Development would impact the wildlife of the refuge.

At this point you are almost two miles from the parking lot, and for my companions and me it's usually a decision point. Will we do the whole loop, totalling 5.5 miles, or go back from here?

Whatever you do, *don't* venture out onto the mud flats. People (grounded boaters, usually) have walked in the mud, gotten stuck, and died when the tide came in.

If you continue around, you head west for a ways and then come back south (toward the freeway) past the curves of McAllister Creek before finally turning and heading east to the parking lot.

Sometimes there is a detour in this part of the trail, as there can be bald eagles nesting in the refuge, and they are very sensitive to human activity. Fortunately, in this place, humans are also sensitive to the eagles' needs. Part of the refreshment I find at the Nisqually Wildlife Refuge is from the effects of loving, thoughtful stewardship here.

ACCESS: Take the freeway toward Seattle from Olympia, and take Exit 114. Turn left to go under the freeway, then turn right onto the frontage road along the north side of the freeway, and there you are. Or you can drive or bicycle out Martin Way.

The parking lot has the usual warnings about not leaving your possessions visible; it also has portable toilets. Adjacent to the parking lot, there's an information kiosk where you can browse the informative displays, pick up maps of the walks, lists of the wildlife to be found, etc.

It's here that you pay the entry fee of $2 per family; annual passes are available in the office.

Nisqually Wildlife Refuge is open daily during daylight hours. Parts of the trail are closed at times; for example, you can't walk the entire 5.5 mile loop during duck hunting season, even though hunting is allowed only on WA lands outside the Refuge. Parts of the refuge are closed at this time to keep people a good distance from the hunters and to give the waterfowl an area where they can be undisturbed. This season is typically the during the last two weeks in October and then from mid-November to mid-January.

For information about the Nisqually Wildlife Refuge, including volunteer opportunities and the wide range of educational programs available, call the Refuge office at (360) 753-9467, Mon-Fri, 7:30AM — 4PM.

There are a variety of groups working toward greater protection of the Nisqually delta, and I wish them good volunteers, good funding, and terrific success! If you would like to get involved or to make a donation, a good place to contact is the Nisqually Delta Association, PO Box 7444, Olympia, WA 98507, phone (360) 357-3792.

No dogs or other pets are permitted here.

More Walks

There are far more than twelve good walks in the Olympia area. Here is a selection, listed in three categories: Around Olympia, Thurston County North, and Thurston County South. Most parks are open from early in the morning until dusk.

Around Olympia

East-West Greenway

This trail will eventually run from Capitol Lake to Lacey. You can now walk two miles from Eastside Street just south of Wheeler Street (which is itself just south of where Eastside goes over I-5) to Dayton Street and back. This part of the trail follows an old railroad right-of-way, so it's quite level. There are trees on either side. The East-West Greenway Association, a non-profit organization, has worked very hard, along with the city, to make this trail a reality. To get the association's newsletter with a donation, or to find out more, write PO Box 7067, Olympia, WA 98507 or call 786-9233. They offer guided walks.

Garfield Nature Trail

Garfield Nature Trail is tucked into a hidden ravine on Olympia's Westside. The park is only about a hundred yards wide and a third of a mile long, and it has no bathrooms or other amenities. The trail crosses a creek several times on small bridges, and meanders under tall trees and an old water-pipe trestle. It goes between Rogers Street and West Bay Drive about .75 mile north of Harrison Blvd., and you can park at either end of the trail.

It's such a short walk that I like to do it both ways. West Bay is considerably lower than Rogers, so choose whether you want your uphill walk to be first or last.

Yauger Park

Yauger Park on Olympia's Westside is best known for its ballfields. It also offers a demonstration garden for native plants and composting, and a pretty .75 mile nature trail with interpretive signs. To get there, take 4th across the bridge from downtown. Bear right and it becomes Harrison; continue to Cooper Point Road, a corner with a traffic light. Turn left onto Cooper Point, and you'll soon be passing the ballfields on your right. Take the first right, Capital Mall Drive, and then turn right at Alta Street and go to the end of the street. You're there.

Lacey's Wonderwood Park

This forty-acre park has natural woodlands as well as playing areas and ballfields. It's between College Street and Ruddell Road, north of 32nd Ave.

Tumwater Hill

Head toward the Tumwater water tower for panoramic views that include the Black Hills, Puget Sound, the Olympics, and the State Capitol. You have to lift your eyes above all the housing, but even so it's one of the best views around. There is a small park where you could enjoy a picnic dinner. From I-5, take Hwy 101 and then the Cooper Pt./Crosby Rd. exit. Go left over the freeway and stay on Crosby as it goes uphill. Turn left onto Barnes Blvd. The park is on your right, at the top of the hill, opposite an entrance to "The Peak," one of the apartment complexes. I've seen deer in the woods near the park.

If you like to sweat a bit for your pleasures, you could turn left onto Irving Street from Crosby Road, and then turn right on 12th Avenue. Park in this area, and walk uphill on 12th to Vista Loop. Turn right there, to

Barnes, then left on Barnes and proceed to the park.
Return the same way, or stay on Barnes to Crosby, then go
right on Crosby to Irving, right on it and back to your car.

Thurston County North

Boston Harbor

To get to Boston Harbor, follow the directions for Priest
Point Park and keep on going several miles on the road
that was Plum Street, then East Bay Drive, and
eventually becomes Boston Harbor Road. This hilly, pretty
route has wide shoulders for bikes and pedestrians. Turn
left on 73rd Avenue, and go a couple of blocks to the
Marina, a nice place with outstanding views. Busses come
from downtown Olympia.

You can just
wander around; one
local walker sug-
gested a triangle of
going back toward
town on Boston
Harbor Road to
Zangle Road,

Sailboats race near Boston Harbor.   turning left on
Zangle and taking it to 73rd Avenue, just after the Boston
Harbor Elementary School, and then going left on 73rd
back to the start. She said she avoids this route during the
busier times of day; there aren't sidewalks and not always
much shoulder.

Burfoot County Park

On the way to Boston Harbor, stop at this sixty-acre park
which features trails descending through the woods to a
thousand-foot pebble beach on Budd Inlet. Some of the
stairs are steep. The park also has picnic tables and large
grassy areas; it's a spot that can get busy on hot summer
weekends. Much like Priest Point Park in its plant life, it
too has a bit of poison oak near the shore. In the spring,

I've seen masses of trillium under the trees.

Burfoot Park got its start in 1966 when Archie and Mildred Burfoot sold their land, some nineteen acres, to the county for about a third of what condominium-minded developers had offered them. Every time I go there, I feel grateful to them, especially since the amount of public access to the shores of Puget Sound is minimal.

Chehalis-Western Trail to Woodard Bay

Six miles of trail following an old railroad grade go north from Martin Way to the Woodard Bay Conservation Area. On Martin Way, the trailhead is between Libby Road and Sleater-Kinney Road; when I was there, the parking was minimal. One popular access point is on South Bay Road near its intersection with Lilly Road. There is parking available there, though also limited.

This is a superhighway of a trail. The first half is paved and about ten feet wide, with soft shoulders on either sides. You may see hikers, runners, skaters, bicyclists (including commuters) and horseback riders. On a summer evening, it can be a very sociable place. Just don't choose it if quiet communing with nature is your goal. There are plans to pave all the trail eventually, as funds permit.

At Woodard Bay itself, paths through the deep forest do provide more tranquillity. You can walk to the area once used by the Weyerhaeuser Company as a "log dump". Rail cars brought the logs to the water and dumped them in. Then they were put together in rafts and transported to mills. Tiny one-man tugboats muscled the rafts around. Harbor seals, blue herons, bald eagles, bats, and numerous species of waterfowl inhabit the area. Bicycling, horseback riding and other activities that would disturb the animals are not appropriate here.

To drive or bicycle to Woodard Bay, go north on East Bay Drive (which becomes Boston Harbor Road) several miles past Priest Point Park to Woodard Bay Road. Turn right on it; go left where it becomes Libby Road, and then turn right on Woodard Bay Road. The parking area is on the left before the road crosses the water.

Frye Cove County Park

This small park provides waterfront access to Eld Inlet and lovely views of Mt. Rainier. It is best enjoyed at a low tide. There is a two-mile trail through forests and wetlands. It's a new park—opened in 1992 —and yet to be discovered by many people, so it's a tranquil place to enjoy the characteristic woods, ferns, and water views of this region. The shore, about .3 mile long, is a good place to launch kayaks and canoes. To get there, take Highway 101 toward Shelton, turn right on Steamboat Island Road, then after about a mile turn right on Gravelly Beach Rd, stay on it about two miles to Young Rd., turn left on Young, then right on 61st to the park entrance. Admission is free.

Most children love to explore; here, Clare Bellefeuille-Rice is the first to notice a bird at Frye Cove.

Tolmie State Park

Tolmie provides a lovely shallow beach on Nisqually Reach that is about 1800 feet long and safe for young children. It also has over three miles of hiking trails; the main loop trail is about two and a quarter miles. There is poison oak here, though I don't recall seeing it right on the trail. To get there take I-5 north of Olympia to exit 111. Head north on Marvin Road to Johnson Point Road.

Thurston County South:

Deschutes Falls Park

This remote park, operated by the Thurston County Parks Department, provides beautiful views of two Deschutes River falls, a twenty-seven-foot and a thirty-five-foot, plus picnic areas in a wooded setting. It was a private park from the early 1900s until relatively recently. This park is at the end of Bald Hills Road, which you can get on at the edge of Yelm.

Millersylvania State Park

This 841-acre park offers several miles of trails including a 1.5 mile exercise trail with twenty workout stations. It can be very crowded during the summer, with campers drawn to the sites under the tall trees and swimmers drawn to a shallow swim area on Deep Lake, so Millersylvania is best enjoyed during the less crowded months. To reach it, go south on I-5 to exit 95, east for two miles, then north on Tilley Road for a mile. Day use is free. In the 1930s, it was the site of a CCC Camp, and there are some lovely old shelters and buildings from that project. This park is one of the main travellers' destinations in Thurston County.

Tenino

Tenino is a small town that has not yet seen the explosive growth that has so changed the Olympia area. Its sandstone has provided materials for buildings throughout the West as well as for many buildings still standing in downtown Tenino. Well-known local stonecutter Keith Phillips has added a variety of delightful sandstone works to the town in recent years.

To reach Tenino, follow Old Highway 99 (Capitol Way) south from Olympia or take I-5 south to the Tenino exit. In July, the town hosts the Tenino Oregon Trail Days on a weekend.

You can start a walk at the city park, which has a museum made from an old train depot and a very unusual

and attractive swimming pool, made from an old sandstone quarry and fed by cool natural springs. From there,
walk over on Olympia Street to Sussex Street. Most of the
interesting old buildings are to your left, in the next couple
of blocks on both sides of Sussex. There's a walking tour
brochure listed in the Resource Guide.

Wolf Haven

Wolf Haven is an exceptionally interesting and worthwhile
place that offers a walking tour, but it's not actually a
walk. Located on sixty-five acres south of Olympia, Wolf
Haven was founded in 1982 as a haven for abandoned or
captive-born wolves that cannot be placed in the wilds. It
provides permanent homes for about forty wolves kept in
large enclosures. Wolf Haven plays a significant role in
educating the public about wolves. I certainly learned a
lot, including the fact that wolves can see a moving animal
three miles away!

Wolf Haven is reached by taking I-5 south to exit
99, then going east on 93rd Ave. At the intersection with
Old 99, turn right and go south 3.5 miles. Turn left on
Offutt Lake Road to the Wolf Haven sign. Call Intercity
Transit for bus access. Wolf Haven is on the way to
Tenino; both together make a good outing.

There is an entrance fee, a well-stocked gift shop,
an adopt-a-wolf program, and lots of volunteer opportunities. Open hours vary with the seasons. In summer
(May-Sept.), it's daily 10AM—5PM; the rest of the year,
it's open Wednesday through Sunday and they close an
hour earlier. For more information call (360) 264-4695.

And More, and More, and More...

Mt Rainier... the world-famous Olympic Peninsula...
Pacific beaches... Seattle and Tacoma, with their myriad
urban possibilities... the volcano, Mt. St. Helens, with
very informative visitors' centers... the beautiful San Juan
Islands... Canada... There's always more!

Resource Guide

I hope I've whetted your appetite for more tales and background on this region. Many of these items are available in local bookstores; for those that are out of print, the Timberland Regional Library probably has copies, or you might get lucky at the used bookstores.

Articles

Amberson, Susan, and Bruce Fortune. "The Nisqually, A Delta Under Fire," *Underwater Naturalist*, Bulletin of the American Littoral Society, Vol. 21, No. 1, May 1992, pp. 24-27.

Berg, Andrew W. "Formation of Mima Mounds: A Seismic Hypothesis," *Geology*, Vol. 18, March 1990, pp. 281-284. The latest geological theory. I was leaning toward the mole theory till I read this.

Cox, George W. "Mounds of Mystery," *Natural History*, June 1984, pp. 36-44. Article putting forth the gopher theory for the Mima Mounds. Also briefly describes some geological theories and presents arguments against them.

Duncan, Don. "Mystery of Mima Mounds," *Seattle Times*, Feb. 5, 1984, p. G4. Describes both theories of Mima Mounds.

McBride, Del. "Nisqually: A Land and Its Original People," *Underwater Naturalist*, Bulletin of the American Littoral Society, Vol. 21, No. 1, May 1992, pp. 22-23.

Scheffer, Victor B. "A Case of Prairie Pimples," *Pacific Discovery*, April-June 1984, pp. 4-8. Article about the gopher theory of the Mima Mounds, by one of the proponents of the theory.

Books And Booklets:

Arender, Barney. *Barney's Book on the Olympic Peninsula: A Compendium for Motorists and Hikers of All Major Roads and Trails*. Olympia: Nosado Press, 2nd ed., 1993. This detailed book describes many walks in the Olympics.

Bigelow, Mary Ann. *Where the Potholes Are*. Olympia: Thurston Regional Planning Council, 1990. Vivid descriptions of early Olympia, enjoyable for both adults and children.

Blumenson, John J.-G. *Identifying American Architecture: A Pictorial Guide to Styles and Terms, 1600-1945*. New York: Norton, 1981. Small book, easy to carry with you.

Dean, Jana. *Sound Wisdom: Stories of Place*. Olympia: Puget Sound Water Quality Authority, 1993. The four tales are good reading or listening for children and adults. Includes discussion of the storytelling process and the sense of place.

Dodds, Gordon B. *The American Northwest: A History of Oregon and Washington.* Arlington Hts, IL: The Forum Press, 1986. Good background reading.

Felt, Margaret Elly. *Capitol Forest ... the Forest that Came Back.* Olympia: Washington Department of Natural Resources, 1975. I found this at the state library. Background on the forest.

Goff, Susan. *Tenino Sandstone: A Walking Tour of Tenino's Sandstone Buildings and Sites.* Tenino, WA: Tenino Chamber of Commerce and South Thurston County Historical Society.

How the West was Once: A History of West Olympia. By Larry Smith's Eighth Grade English classes. Olympia: Jefferson Junior High, 1974. I found this gem at the library and drew on it for my Westside chapter. Too bad it's not still in print.

Johnston, Norman J. *Washington's Audacious State Capitol and Its Builders.* University of Washington Press, 1988. Lots of detail and history, lavishly illustrated.

Kirk, Ruth, and Carmela Alexander. *Exploring Washington's Past: A Road Guide to History.* Seattle: University of Washington Press, 1990. Fun to travel with!

Koenninger, Robin Bragg. *Here in God's Country... A Celebration of South Sound: Its People, Places, and Pleasurable Pastimes.* Olympia: 1991, Percival Press. A potpourri about the region from a popular writer for the *Olympian.*

Manning, Harvey and Penny. *Footsore 4: Walks and Hikes Around Puget Sound.* Seattle: The Mountaineers, 1990, 2nd ed. Describes many walks in the southern Puget Sound region, with maps, photos, and a personable style.

Mueller, Marge and Ted. *South Puget Sound Afoot and Afloat.* Seattle: The Mountaineers, 1991, 2nd ed. Similar to the book by the Mannings but with a lot of different information.

Mueller, Marge and Ted. *Washington State Parks: A Complete Recreation Guide.* Seattle: The Mountaineers, 1993. Includes description of Millersylvania State Park near Olympia.

Newell, Gordon, *Rogues, Buffoons, and Statesmen.* Seattle: Hangman Press/Superior Publishing, 1975. Over 500 pages of informative and hilarious details of capital characters and the city.

Newell, Gordon R. *So Fair a Dwelling Place: A History of Olympia and Thurston County, Washington.* Olympia: Warren's Printing and Graphic Arts, 1984. Interesting history with photos. Both of Newell's books are out of print but in libraries.

Nicandri, David, and Derek Valley. *Olympia Wins: Washington's Capital Controversies.* Olympia: Washington State Capitol Museum, 1980. Entertaining description of the infighting between Washington cities over where the capitol would be located, with a number of old photographs.

Nicandri, David. *Olympia's Forgotten Pioneers: The Oblates of Mary Immaculate.* Olympia: State Capitol Historical Association, 1976. The tale of the founders of Priest Point Park.

Palmer, Gayle, and Shanna Stevenson. *Thurston County Place Names: A Heritage Guide.* Olympia: Thurston County Historic Commission, 1992. List of places, with description, history, and meanings of the names. Dozens of illustrations, mostly old photographs. Useful for researchers, and enjoyable browsing.

Patterson, Nancy. *South Sound Places: A Guide to Olympia, Lacey, Tumwater, and Thurston County.* Olympia: Four Seasons Publishing, 1993. A compendium of information, covering many things that my book doesn't.

Petersen, Keith C., and Mary E. Reed. *Discovering Washington: A Guide to State and Local History.* Pullman: Washington State University Press, 1989. Describes organizations and libraries (several in Olympia) that can help you do research.

Stevenson, Shanna, et al., *Downtown Olympia's Historic Resources.* Olympia: Olympia Heritage Commission, 1984. Many details in the downtown chapter came from here.

Stevenson, Shanna, and Thomas Constantini. *Olympia Cultural Resources Inventory.* Olympia: Washington State Office of Archaeology and Historic Preservation, 1986. Includes historical background, lists of properties surveyed, and more.

Stevenson, Shanna, and Thomas Constantini. *Olympia Cultural Resources Inventory: Downtown Inventoried Properties.* Olympia: Washington State Office of Archaeology and Historic Preservation, 1986.

Stevenson, Shanna, *Lacey, Olympia, and Tumwater: A Pictorial History.* Norfolk, VA: Donning Co., 1985. If I could have one book on local history, it would be this one. Presently out of print; available in libraries. A fine blend of lively text and historic photos.

Stevenson, Shanna. *Olympiana: Historical Vignettes of Olympia's People and Places.* Olympia: Washington State Capitol Museum, 1982. Boston Harbor's dreams of glory, the history of the Capitol Theater, and much more comes to life. Many details in the walks came from here.

Stratton, David H. *Washington Comes of Age: The State in the National Experience.* Pullman, WA: Washington State University Press, 1992. A collection of essays: personal, political and historical.

Maps, flyers, and brochures:

There are many things that fall into this category. A trip to the Chamber of Commerce office or the Visitor Center on the State Capitol campus will yield lots of goodies. Here is a selection:

City of Olympia, *Olympia Tourism Guide*. Available at City Hall, on the SW corner of Plum and 8th Ave SE, open Mon.-Fri., 8-5.

Department of Natural Resources (DNR), State of WA. Map, "Capitol State Forest and Lower Chehalis State Forest." 1995. This is a newer edition than the map I used. Available from WA Dept of Natural Resources (DNR). You can send $1.08 check or money order to DNR, Photo and Map Sales, Box 47031, Olympia, WA 98504-7031, and they will mail it to you within 30 days, often much faster. Or you can go by the DNR building on the State Capitol campus (see map on Walk #1), and pick up a copy of the map, also for $1.08, Mon.-Fri., 8:30 -4:30. They also have a wonderful selection of interesting maps and aerial photos. (360) 902-1234.

Jacobsen, Arthur Lee. *Trees of the Washington State Capitol*. Olympia: Washington State House of Representatives, 1993. Free brochure describes twenty types of trees on the campus, with a walking tour. Available at the State Capitol Visitor Center.

Olympia Heritage Commission, City of Olympia. Series of free walking tour brochures. *Bigelow Neighborhood, Historic Downtown Olympia, South Capitol Neighborhood. West Side Neighborhood.* I drew on these for my walks. A newer one, *Southeast Neighborhood,* I haven't seen yet. These are very attractive and informative, with lots of old photos and many details that I didn't include. Available at Olympia City Hall and the State Capitol Visitor Center. For more information, call (360) 786-5745.

Newspapers:

The Olympian. This daily newspaper includes many articles about city history, politics, things to do, etc. Widely available; I found it extremely useful in learning about the community. Robin Koenninger often tells interesting people stories; there is good travel writing; and the back page of the front section describes local events coming up. Every summer, the newspaper publishes a special supplement, *The Sourcebook: A South Sound Guide for Newcomers and Natives.* Each year, it also publishes a free booklet of daily tides, handy for planning beach and boating activities. Subscription phone, (360) 754-5411.

South Sound Green Pages. Olympia: South Puget Sound Environmental Education Clearing House (S.P.E.E.C.H), free monthly with lots of news about the natural world. $20 memberships mailed to 218 W 4th Ave, Olympia WA 98501 will get the newsletter mailed to you. (360) 786-6349

Other Publications:

Historic Property Inventory Forms. Olympia: Thurston Regional Planning Council. Available for historic buildings and sites throughout the county, these informative pages provided details for many of my walks, especially downtown.

Johnson, Marlan. *Eastside History*. A paper written a few years ago by an Evergreen student and in the hands of the Board of the Eastside Neighborhood Association, which hopes to publish it.

Places to Get Information:

Capital Volkssport Club has year-round walking (and bicycling) groups. There's a walk that starts at the Deli of the Bayview Market. For more information about this group, call (360) 877-5461.

The City of Olympia has a phone recording describing what's going on; call (360) 753-8262.

F.I.S.T. (Feminists in Self-Defense Training) offer classes in self-defense for women of all ages and backgrounds. I found the teachers very respectful of what each woman felt comfortable doing. Call (360) 438-0288.

Olympia-Thurston County Chamber of Commerce, 521 Legion Way, Olympia (a few blocks east of Sylvester Park). (360) 357-3362. Open Mon.-Fri., 9-5. Information and brochures.

Olympia Timberland Library, 313 8th Ave SE, Olympia, on the edge of downtown, a block south of the old Carnegie library (see downtown map.) Phone (360) 352-0595. Part of the multi-county Timberland public library system.

State Capitol Visitor Center, corner of Capitol Way and 14th., (360) 586-3460. Open 8AM-5PM Mon.-Fri. all year, and from Memorial Day to Labor Day also open Sat-Sun 10AM-4PM, will mail out information.

U. S. West telephone book: maps, descriptions of community events, etc., between the white and yellow pages.

Videotape

Exploring Olympia: Washington's Capital City. Produced by Kelly Hart, 22 minutes. Olympia: Hartworks, 1995. This was created by my husband, who collected video footage at many community events, such as Bon Odori and the pet parade, as well as at the places you'd expect in a travel video of Olympia.

Index

Colophon

Twelve Walks Around Olympia was written and formatted in Word for Windows 6.0c, running on a 486 computer. True Type fonts were used: Century Schoolbook, 10.5 point, for the text, and Lucida Sans in various sizes for the headings. Lucida Sans Italic was used for the captions.

The maps were drawn in Coreldraw3, based on scanned-in public domain maps. They just wouldn't go into Word without too many quirks and huge file sizes, so they were pasted up. Coreldraw3 was also used for the cover.

The illustrations were created from photographs taken by Rosana and Kelly Hart, except for the ones on pages 17, 31, 37, 39, and 71, which were from the collection of Roger Easton. Also, the illustration on page 79 is from the Bigelow family collection, and was scanned in, with permission, from an issue of the Olympia Food Coop's *Coop News*.

Photographs, whether black and white or color, were scanned in with a Logitech hand scanner as black-and-white line art, then cropped and sized in FotoTouch Color and imported into Word.

Output was to an Epson ActionLaser 1400, with 600x600 dpi resolution. Printing was by Gorham Printing, Rochester, WA.

Also Available from Hartworks

VIDEOTAPES

Exploring Olympia: Washington's Capital City. Videotape, 22 minutes, 1995, produced by Kelly Hart (as are all these videotapes). $19.95 plus $2.00 shipping and handling. Shows the beautiful buildings and scenery you'd expect, and also brings out the human side of Olympia, with festivals and musicians. Local people tell us they are sending it to relatives who haven't been to Olympia.

Mexican Pizza: Lively Conversations in Spanish, with booklet containing translations. $35 plus $2 shipping. 24 mins. Train your ear as you follow the spontaneous conversation of a group of vivacious students.

Student Life in Mexico, Featuring Emilio Delgado. $29.95 plus $2 shipping. 18 mins. Visit Mexican children in their classrooms, at home, at work, and at play. For grade 3 to adult. Commentary by a popular children's television personality.

Telepathic Communication with Animals, featuring Penelope Smith. $29.95 plus $2 shipping. Have you ever wished you knew what an animal was thinking? Penelope talks with them easily.

The Tellington TTouch for Happier, Healthier Cats, featuring Linda Tellington-Jones. $29.95 plus $2 shipping.

The Tellington TTouch for Happier, Healthier Dogs, featuring Linda Tellington-Jones. $29.95 plus $2 shipping.
These two programs present a unique way of touching your animals, by the woman who invented it. It often has remarkable effects on the health and well-being of animals.

Why Llamas? $19.95 plus $2 shipping. Delightful, fast-paced introduction to llamas. With the Andean music of Sukay.

BOOKS

Living with Llamas: Tales from Juniper Ridge. By Rosana Hart. 192pp., third edition, 1991. $11.95 plus $2 shipping. Personal, informative account of our years with llamas.

Llamas for Love and Money. By Rosana Hart. 176 pp. Second edition, 1994. $14.95 plus $2 shipping. Acclaimed introduction to all aspects of llama care as well as the business of llamas.

Order Form

(If you are in the Olympia area, you can purchase this book, our llama books, and our Olympia videotape at a variety of stores and save the shipping charges.)

HOW MANY	TITLE	PRICE incl. shpg	TOTAL
	12 Walks Around Olympia (this book)	$14.00	
	Exploring Olympia (Videotape)	$21.95	
	SPECIAL, Set of Olympia book and video, save $4.95	$31.00	
	Catalog of Juniper Ridge Press llama books and videos	FREE	FREE
	Above prices include 4th class shipping. Add $1.50 to your whole order for priority mail.		
	For orders shipped to WA addresses, add 7.9% state sales tax.		
		TOTAL:	

PLEASE PRINT LEGIBLY

NAME:

ADDRESS:

CITY, STATE, ZIP:

Check, money order, MasterCard, and Visa welcomed. Make checks (US funds) payable to Hartworks. Call us for information on quantity discounts.

If you are paying with a credit card, is it MC?___ Visa?___
Card #:
Expiration date:
Your phone number, with area code:
Signature:

Send to: Hartworks, PO Box 1278, Olympia, WA 98507
Phone (360) 705-1328, FAX (360) 357-9049;
Non-local order line, (800) 869-7342.